Black in the White House

Black in the White House

Life Inside George W. Bush's West Wing

Ron Christie

NELSON CURRENT

A Subsidiary of Thomas Nelson, Inc.

www.NelsonCurrent.com

Published in Nashville, Tennessee, by Nelson Current, a division of a wholly-owned subsidiary (Nelson Communications, Inc.) of Thomas Nelson, Inc.

Nelson Current books may be purchased in bulk for educational, business, fundraising, or sales promotional use. For information, please e-mail SpecialMarkets@ThomasNelson.com.

Map of West Wing on pages xii and xiii are provided by the *Washington Post* and used by permission.

Library of Congress cataloging-in-publication data on file with the Library of Congress.

ISBN 1-59555-039-9

Printed in the United States of America

06 07 08 09 10 QW 5 4 3 2 1

To Jennifer Kay Christie,
my best friend and love of my life

Somewhere ages and ages hence:

Two roads diverged in a wood, and I—

I took the one less traveled by,

And that has made all the difference.

— Robert Frost

TABLE OF CONTENTS

Cast of Characters

The President: Behind the president's often warm and engaging persona is a man with an acerbic sense of humor who is extremely impatient with those not in complete command of their facts and surroundings. At the same time, he takes particular pleasure in getting to know his staff and making them feel comfortable with him. Media accounts of his intellect not withstanding, he has one of the sharpest abilities of anyone I've ever met to remember arcane facts and usually knows far more about any particular subject than the staff that is briefing him.

The Vice President: Often described as the "man behind the man," the vice president is the consummate team player, and his loyalty to President Bush is unparalleled. He is accurately described as the president's consigliere, deploying himself in town and around the world whenever and wherever necessary to advance the Bush agenda. A reserved, affable man away from the public eye, the vice president is someone with whom I formed a special bond that allowed us to engage in candid conversations about race relations and how it feels to be a black man living in America today.

Andy Card: Thoughtful, unassuming, and extremely intelligent, Andy Card is the glue that keeps the ship together—the man who makes the trains run on time in the Bush White House. While polite and engaging with staff around the White House, Card often assumes the role of the "bad cop" to the president's "good cop," ensuring that none of the president's precious business, social, or personal time is wasted. Unprepared staff sometimes find themselves on the wrong side of his Yankee-clipped, stoic New England temperament. Along with the vice president, Card took an active role in working with me to explore ways to present the president's agenda to people of color because it was the right thing, rather than the politically expedient thing, to do.

Karl Rove: Often called Bush's brain, the deputy chief of staff and senior advisor is the political mastermind under whose microscope every presidential activity is minutely examined to ensure maximum political and media advantage. Rove can often be found refilling the water glasses of unsuspecting guests in the White House Mess, teasing staff from the most senior to junior levels, and serving as the "Mayor" of the West Wing, but behind Rove's jovial disposition is a man of extraordinary intellect, discipline, and work ethic. Though he is engaging in social settings, his rebukes cut like a lance to those cabinet secretaries and staff who fail to demonstrate comprehensive knowledge of their subject matter when victimized by one of Rove's pop quizzes. His empire comprises the Office of Strategic Initiatives, Political Affairs, Inter-Governmental Affairs, Public Liaison, and the Office of Faith-Based and Community Initiatives, a formidable network of loyal staff and confidantes who keep him up to date on the latest "buzz" inside and outside of the White House.

Mary Matalin: The late Lee Atwater's bright, quirky acolyte is perhaps best known for her marriage to the "Raging Cajun," Democratic consultant James Carville. Matalin is one of only two staff members who served President Bush and the vice president at the same time while I was in the administration, and she has the best pure instincts in assessing situations and explaining difficult concepts of anyone I've ever known. She's also the only staff person brave enough to look the vice president in the eye and say, "Now that's a dumb idea," without evoking any reaction from him other than laughter. Matalin took a particular interest in my development as a Bush loyalist and as an individual, once describing me as the son she never had. She is the true "Compassionate Conservative," with no tolerance for racial insensitivity—particularly after a senior member of the vice president's staff described our racially diverse policy office as a "ghetto."

Scooter Libby: The man most instrumental to my joining the Bush administration. Wading through a sea of résumés and recommendations from well-connected big shots, Libby called me in Florida just after the recount had ended to ask me to come in for an interview. As the vice president's chief of staff, Scooter was responsible for hiring a calm, smart, and loyal staff to support the vice president's voracious appetite for information. Scooter established a working environment in which one's value to the team was measured by the quality, not the quantity, of one's work (read: the number of hours one's butt remained in a chair). The utterly unflappable Scooter was a pillar of stability after the 9/11 attacks, providing sage counsel to the VP while ensuring the most junior staffer's nerves were calmed. A true gentleman.

The West Wing

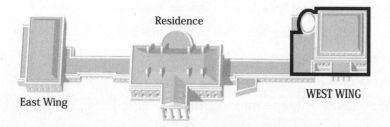

Residence

East Wing

WEST WING

FIRST FLOOR

1 Blake Gottesman, personal aide

2 Karen Keller, personal secretary

3 Scott McClellan, press secretary

4 Vacant

5 Erin Healy, assistant press secretary

6 J.D. Crouch II, deputy national security adviser

7 Stephen J. Hadley, national security adviser

8 Vice President Cheney

9 Michael J. Gerson, assistant to the president for policy and strategic planning

10 Susan Ralston, assistant to the senior adviser

Steve Atkiss, special assistant to the president for operations

11 Joseph Hagin, deputy chief of staff

12 Karl Rove, deputy chief of staff/senior adviser

13 Andrew H. Card Jr., chief of staff

SECOND FLOOR

14 Dan Bartlett, counselor

15 Nicolle Devenish, assistant to the president for communications

16 Candi Wolff, legislative director

17 Doug Badger, deputy legislative director

18 Allan B. Hubbard, National Economic Council director

19 Keith Hennessey, National Economic Council deputy director

20 William McGurn, chief speechwriter

21 Dina Powell, personnel director

22 William Kelley, deputy White House counsel

23 Claude Allen, domestic policy adviser

24 Tevi Troy, deputy domestic policy adviser

25 Kristen Silverberg, adviser to the chief of staff

26 Harriet Miers, White House counsel

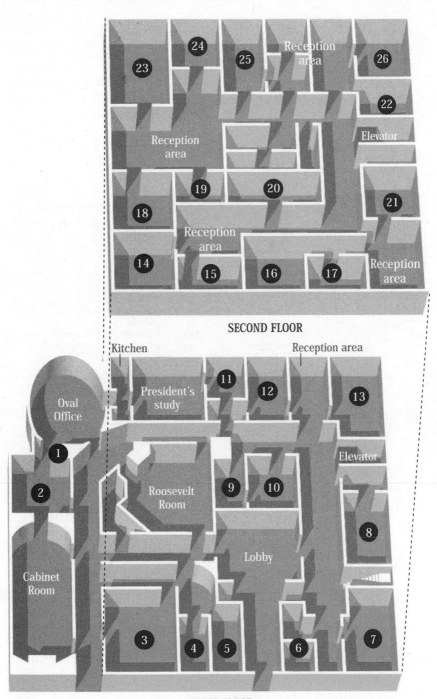

SECOND FLOOR

FIRST FLOOR

Prologue

24 FEBRUARY 2004. I RECEIVED THE PHONE CALL I HAD ONLY dreamt I would receive: The president was going. But first, I had to go and meet with him.

Entering the West Wing, my feet didn't seem to touch the ground as I turned the corner and bounded up the stairs to the first floor of the building. Almost there. Poking my head into the chief of staff's office, I saw Andy Card had already walked down to the Oval Office. Deputy Chief of Staff Harriet Miers, though, greeted me at the door and walked with me the few short steps down the hall. Entering the president's outer office, I was surprised to note that National Security Advisor Condoleezza Rice was there: Who told her the president was going? As if reading my mind, she smiled and told me, "I wasn't going to miss this."

Seconds later, I walked into the Oval Office with Dr. Rice and Harriet Miers right behind me. Card, already in with the president, could do little to mask the beaming expression on his face. Peering over his reading glasses at me, the president asked, "What have we got?"

What we had was the first president of the United States ever to sign legislation that would create a national museum dedicated to the history and culture of African Americans. What we had was a president who was about to join a group of hundreds of celebrants in the East Room of the White House who had gathered not only to commemorate Black History Month with Mr. Bush, but also to celebrate the fact that a nearly hundred-year journey to create a black history museum in Washington D.C. had reached a glorious end.

Like Card, I could barely keep the smile from my face as the president waited for my answer. Walking to the corner of the desk where the president was now standing, I tried to contain my enthusiasm. "Mr. President, you are going to a celebration," I began. "These folks are looking to celebrate with you the fact that you signed a bill into law that has never been done before that will create an African-American Museum in Washington." The president flipped through his remarks and frowned. "I don't see that in here," he said.

Undeterred, I plunged ahead. "Mr. President. Please speak to these folks from your heart. Talk about how happy you are to be there, celebrating the creation of this museum, one that will chronicle the lives of African Americans from times of slavery, Reconstruction, the Harlem Renaissance, and the Civil Rights Era." Like the president, I had seen his printed remarks prepared by the speechwriting office, and while well written, they touched on the war on terrorism, homeland security, and other matters of the day. But this was no ordinary speech, and I was doing all I could to share with the president that he couldn't treat it as such.

Before I joined the Bush administration, I had no idea that the effort to establish a black history museum in Washington D.C. was nearly a hundred years old. Going back to when black veterans, whose valor helped preserve the Union, marched alongside children of slaves in the nation's capital in 1915, the push for public land and space for a museum recognizing the significant achievements of African Americans has been a long and hard fight.

The fight ended on 16 December 2003, when the president signed H.R. 3491 into a law that called for the creation of America's first Museum of African American History and Culture. Despite legislative efforts going back as far as 1929, Congress had never acted to bring such a bill to the floor for a vote and present it to the president for his signature—including the portion of President Clinton's tenure when the Democrats controlled both the House and the Senate.

I wanted President George W. Bush to stand up and take a bow for helping bring this day about, for no other reason than that this was a project so long overdue and the president had put his pen to paper to sign the bill into law, making the dream into a happy reality.

Still peering over his glasses at me, the president said, "Walk with me." With my mouth running a mile a minute, I opened the door from the Oval leading to the Rose Garden, and we slowly walked down the colonnade as the president reflected on what he would say to the gathering that awaited him. Condi Rice, Deputy Chief of Staff Harriet Miers, and personal aide Blake Gottesman trailed behind us, giving us space.

The president asked me once again what I had said a few moments before. With his reading glasses off now, he was giving me his full and undivided attention. While repeating my thoughts about the various struggles and contributions African Americans had made to the history and culture of the United States, I could tell the wheels were whirring in the president's mind. I sensed that the president was now formulating what he wanted to say, and I fell silent to allow him to reflect on his remarks.

At that point, I couldn't help but chuckle to myself. What was the son of two liberal, black parents from Palo Alto, California, doing talking, let alone conducting business with, the president of the United States in the Oval Office? Before I joined the administration in 2001, I never thought I would ever meet, let alone become colleagues with, the likes of Karl Rove, Andy Card, or Condi Rice.

My wife and parents continue to tease me that I was the Forrest Gump of the Bush "43" White House in that my face seemed to pop up frequently in photographs taken from meetings with the president, vice president, and other administration officials at key moments.

How all this happened is a story in and of itself.

My Road to
the White House

DECEMBER 2000. MY UNLIKELY ODYSSEY TO THE INNER sanctum of the most important suite of executive offices in the world began in the most unlikely of places: Jacksonville, Florida. Just weeks before, I had celebrated the grueling election to the United States Senate of George Allen (R-VA), son of the legendary Redskins coach of the same name. I was serving as Allen's deputy policy advisor, and we were blessed that incumbent Senator Chuck Robb had conceded early in the evening on election night. After speaking to one of my friends in Austin, Texas, who was working on the Bush campaign and congratulated me on Allen's victory, I was confident that the campaign staff of Governor George W. Bush would soon embark on a similar emotional whirlwind of celebration and astonishment when the long journey finally ended. How wrong that assumption would turn out to be for my friends in Texas as well as the entire country.

Three weeks later, I returned home to Alexandria, Virginia, rested and warmed by the vacation my brother and I had just enjoyed in Rio de Janeiro. As I walked through my front door, I was greeted by the sound of my phone ringing and an urgent voice on the message recorder: "Ron, this is the RNC [Republican National Committee] calling. We've chartered an emergency flight going to Jacksonville, Florida, in three hours and we need you to be on it." Emergency flight? I hadn't even put down my bag from my trip, and they want me to go to Jacksonville?

Three hours later, with many of my clothes fresh from the dryer, I found myself on a special charter filled with congressional staff, lobbyists, and other Bush loyalists headed to Florida for the recount, round two. On 8 December 2000, the Florida Supreme Court had called for manual ballot recounts in all Florida counties where so-called "under votes" had not been subject to manual tabulation. Given the uncertainty and chaos surrounding the counting of dimpled and hanging chads in Miami-Dade and Palm Beach Counties, the Bush campaign was taking no chances on whether or not the U.S. Supreme Court would step in to stop further hand recounts: The campaign immediately dispatched Republican recount teams to be on the ground should the mischief recommence.

Immediately upon our arrival at the hotel, we went up to our rooms and descended as one to take up shop in the lobby prior to our first meeting. For many, this gathering was the first time they had been reunited since their original recount adventures. High-fives and hugs were exchanged, and laughter rang out as chad stories from the first recount were relived and embellished.

After we settled in, we moved to the Recount War Room (otherwise known as the hotel ballroom) where team and geographical assignments were distributed. The room looked just as I had imagined: televisions tuned to the cable news networks on either side of the room, a loud (and marginally functional) copy machine in the corner, and telephones all around.

After people took their seats, we were officially welcomed and thanked for coming to the Northern Florida Bush Recount Headquarters at the last minute. The leadership noted that our role at that point was akin to a batter waiting in the on-deck circle. We were to be ready for deployment at a moment's notice, but as yet no demands were placed upon us other than to ensure Governor Bush's votes were fairly and legally counted if we were sent into the field. Given my training as a lawyer, I was asked to be the legal observer of our recount team. I was a rookie to the game of examining punch card ballots, so I was grouped with five veterans from the first recount down south who could show me the ropes in a hurry should the count resume.

My team included a trio of senior Senate aides—Chase Hutto, Geoff Gray, and Matthew Kirk—and I was happy to see that a good friend of mine from the House Judiciary Committee, Steve Pinkos, had joined us, as well as Shawn Vassell, a lobbyist from a well-known Washington D.C. law firm. Immediately upon our dismissal from the recount team meeting, my new teammates and I took stock of our current situation.

Everyone agreed that they were down in Florida to be a part of history and help Governor Bush become the next lawfully elected president of the United States. I was struck by the esprit de corps of my group: Rather than discuss who might get what job in a potential Bush administration, my friends were quite focused on what we would need to do should the Supreme Court permit hand ballot counts to resume. Stories they had shared with me that night about the initial recount in south Florida had shocked me. There were demonstrations by partisans of Vice President Gore and Governor Bush that had escalated into insult-slinging and shoving matches. Once inside the recount rooms, my teammates had witnessed election officials who "helped" discern the intent of voters to cast their ballots for Vice President Gore in a less than democratic manner. In short, I was warned to expect the unexpected and to be ready for anything.

Fortunately, not too long after our arrival, the event we had all been waiting for finally arrived, and we sprang into action. Over the course of the evening on 12 December 2000, we received word that the Supreme Court was about to release its final opinion in the matter of *Bush v. Gore*. For me, this message was particularly poignant as I was down in Florida as our team's legal adviser. Would I have to analyze anything, or would the serious heavy hitters be making all the tough decisions?

Almost as soon as the cable networks announced the Supreme Court had issued its opinion, our fax machine at campaign headquarters hummed to life, agonizingly spitting out one page of the opinion at a time. Fortunately for me, even a cursory reading of the first page told us all we needed to know. By a 7-2 vote, the Justices held that further recounting of ballots by hand would offend the Equal Protection Rights enshrined in the Fourteenth Amendment. Game, set, match to now President-Elect Bush!

After cheering, hugging, and whooping it up for several minutes, the Recount Leadership Team assembled everyone to thank them for sacrificing their time and efforts to help President-Elect Bush. We were then told we would meet again in the morning and that flight arrangements would be made to get everyone back to Washington D.C. in short order. As fate would have it, I would be leaving town a bit earlier than the rest of my teammates.

Earlier in the day, I had received a message from a Scooter Libby—a name that was entirely unfamiliar to me. He had left word that he was calling from the Bush-Cheney Transition Office and was interested in speaking with me about a position once everything down in Florida had been settled. Long before the Supreme Court issued the final opinion that ultimately concluded the 2000 presidential election, the Bush-Cheney Transition Office was well up and running. Located in a nondescript building near the home of transition head Vice President-Elect Dick

Cheney, staff were already preparing cabinet secretary candidates selected by the president-elect for their upcoming Senate confirmation hearings. Additionally, folks were hard at work turning campaign policy promises into position papers that could be dissected and discussed by the president's policy team once the doors opened for the Bush White House, now only several weeks away. Apparently, finding policy staff not already burned out by the grueling campaign was paramount on the priority list of the senior leadership at Transition Headquarters.

Later that evening, Mr. Libby rang again. To be honest, I was wondering who the heck Scooter Libby was in the first place, as he had never clarified his role or position. In short, Libby asked me whether I might be able to meet within the next few days to discuss potential openings in OVP (The Office of the Vice President) with him. Of course I could!

16 December 2000. Back home in my condo in Alexandria, Virginia, for only the second time in the better part of a month, I threw down my bags from the legal recount in Florida and headed for the shower. To say I was nervous was a polite understatement. While Mr. Libby sounded pleasant and friendly on the phone, I got the sense that I would only have one chance to make a good impression.

During the twenty-minute drive to McLean, I kept telling myself that I could only tell them what I knew. Any attempt to BS at this level would be a sure ticket to the exit without hope of a return visit. Pulling into the lot behind the Transition Headquarters, I was startled to see several black SUVs parked with their motors running and earnest looking men peering out the open windows—my introduction to the United States Secret Service. My first glimpse of the Secret Service agents drove home the point that I was about to embark on a journey that, if successful, would put me in close proximity to some of the most powerful and important people in the world. Great, I thought, no pressure at all.

I passed through the security checkpoint and metal detector manned by several pleasant, but thorough, Secret Service agents, and thought, *I am on the other side of the looking glass. Now what?* I was met by Ashley Snee, a friendly staffer from California who had served on the president's campaign staff. After exchanging small talk about our home state, she directed me to a seat on the second floor and returned to her desk. Before me were three doors with computer-generated nametags identifying their occupants. If my memory serves me correctly, from left to right they read: Rove, Libby, Secretary Cheney. Who was this Libby fellow, anyway?

While contemplating the answer to that question, Libby's door opened, and he ushered me inside. Mr. Libby had a warm, engaging face, but I was immediately struck by the power of his eyes. His gaze was probing and steady. I had the distinct impression (one that would later be borne out time and time again) that this man didn't miss much and could spot BS in a nanosecond. And just like that, Libby (he insisted I call him "Scooter") started my interview.

Rather than question my credentials on the Hill or discuss the tactics we employed during former Governor and current U.S. Senator George Allen's (R-VA) successful ouster of incumbent Senator Chuck Robb (D-VA), Scooter asked me about my favorite works of literature and what it was like to play varsity cricket for Haverford College in Pennsylvania. *He wants to talk about literature and cricket? I must be doomed,* I thought to myself. My favorite book? *Snow Falling on Cedars* by David Guterson. Why? I discussed the masterful way the author had spun a fascinating tale of love, discrimination against Japanese Americans during World War II, and a murder trial that would keep Perry Mason fans on the edge of their seats.

We continued our conversation by discussing Philadelphia, growing up on the West Coast, and other important matters, such as our favorite tequila (after a bad experience in college, I was happy to say I didn't have one). In short, for the better part of an hour we discussed everything except why I wanted to join the Bush administration.

Almost as an afterthought, Scooter noted that he had been asked by the vice president-elect to help staff the various offices with policy experts to carry out President Bush's agenda. At this point, Scooter confessed even he didn't know whether or not he would be offered a position himself (an assertion I didn't entirely believe).

We talked about my potential areas of interest before Scooter decided that I might be a stronger addition to the OVP team in domestic policy. "OVP?" I asked. "Office of the Vice President," he responded. When he asked if that would interest me, I nearly fell out of my chair.

After promising to immediately fax an updated copy of my résumé, writing samples, and a condensed list of references, I was about to head out the door when Scooter asked a question while leveling those laser-beam eyes right at me: "What have you ever done that would embarrass the president and vice president? Drinking problems, disciplinary problems, anything? Have you done anything that if uncovered and displayed on the front page of the *Washington Post* would bring discredit and/or embarrassment to the fledgling administration?" I told Scooter that, save for a few parking tickets from the über-efficient Washington D.C. meter maid brigade, I hadn't run afoul of the law. College pranks and the sort, well, that was a different story. After being assured that all was well, I left the Transition Office fairly optimistic that a job offer would be forthcoming any day. For his part, Scooter had even provided me with the names of a few books that he thought I might enjoy.

Visions of White House grandeur filled my head. Which character from Aaron Sorkin's *The West Wing* would I most likely resemble? I settled on a cross between Sam Seaborn and Josh Lyman: smart, witty, always armed with the right answer! How soon would it be before I was hobnobbing with the president and helping him tackle tough domestic policy challenges? Oh, it went on and on. There was only one little problem. Just as soon as I had faxed Scooter the promised background information that day, I was treated to a little of Simon and Garfunkel's "Sounds of Silence." No return phone call from Scooter, no return e-mail, no nothing.

Had I blown the interview after all? Should I have elected to talk more about politics than contemporary American fiction? Would my only visit to the White House now come as part of the East Wing public tour? These and Lord knows how many other insecure thoughts raced through my mind as I waited for my phone to ring and my e-mail inbox to announce the receipt of a new message. One day slipped into another, and soon a week had passed. Having heard nothing to this point, I began to fear the worst.

Several days later came a glimmer of hope. Cesar Conda, chief of staff to the recently defeated Senator Spencer Abraham (R-MI) (and soon-to-be-announced nominee for secretary of energy), had called to ask about my interview with Scooter. Apparently, Cesar was in line to command the VP's Domestic Policy Office, and, unbeknownst to me, Scooter had asked Cesar to call and "feel me out." We talked for quite some time about our respective backgrounds and swapped war stories from the Hill. As it turned out, one of his former staffers was a member of my recount team from Florida, and I immediately wondered if I had stiff competition from all corners. Cesar told me that he had heard that the next step in the process would be a one-on-one visit with Cheney himself. Placing the phone down, I wondered how long I would have to wait.

As it turned out, not long. A day or so later, Cesar called to tell me he was about to go in to meet with VP-Elect Cheney. Still nervous after having not heard back from Scooter or anyone else over at Transition, I wondered if my candidacy was still alive. A few hours later, Cesar phoned back and spilled the dirt. He said that he and Cheney had spoken at length about politics, the election, and what the administration had hoped to accomplish on domestic issues. All in all, Cesar felt pretty confident about the impression he had made on the president-elect's closest advisor. I wondered how long it would take for me, if at all, to get my shot as well.

Almost immediately after Cesar and I had clicked off, I got the call I had been waiting for (okay, obsessing over). The vice president-elect would like to see me soon. I couldn't believe it! Had I made it? I was so excited that I went over to the nearby Pentagon City shopping mall to purchase a new tie, but I didn't see anything worthy of this particular interview. The best I could do to dress for success was to put such a shine on my shoes that VP-Elect Cheney would be able to see his own reflection in them.

9 January 2001. Armed in the battlegear of the Washington Republican lawyer/lobbyist (starched white shirt, conservative tie, charcoal gray suit, black lace-ups), I arrived at the official Presidential Transition Office Suite located just a stone's throw from the White House at 17th and G. Street N.W. In the weeks following the Supreme Court decision, the Bush-Cheney team had moved from McLean, Virginia, to the set of offices officially designated for use by the incoming administration, just down the street from the Old Executive Office Building. Almost there, but not quite.

In contrast to the handful of vehicles containing Secret Service agents at the McLean facility, the street in front of the D.C. Transition Office looked like a crime scene from *C.S.I.* For one, there were Metropolitan police cars stationed up and down the block. Where there weren't cop cars parked, the Secret Service had placed their own squad cars, along with the ubiquitous black SUVs with the engines running. As if that weren't enough, there were several TV news vans with their lights blazing and antennae stretched up far in the air. No worries, no pressure, I thought to myself. Here we go again. The biggest test in my professional career lay on the other side of those revolving glass doors, and this time I felt surprisingly confident, unlike the package of bundled nerves that arrived in McLean for the first go-around.

Breezing through the security checkpoint like a seasoned veteran, I strode to the elevator, filled with a strong sense of mission and purpose. I told myself time and time again that Mr. Cheney wouldn't waste his time on me if he weren't interested. All I needed to do was take a deep breath, answer his questions while managing to look at him one or two times, and hope that I would get the chance to impress him with my qualifications. Even if I failed, I would be proud of myself for at least making it to this point.

Yeah, right. If I made it this far and failed to get a job, I would be crushed. Devastated. Totally bummed out. There, much better. Nerves completely on edge. Now, let the games begin.

Whisked up several floors in the Transition Headquarters, I was escorted to a set of suites that contained the vice president-elect's personal office. Along the way, I saw people in the halls straight from the television screen. Around the bend and there was Ari Fleischer, the campaign spokesman and incoming White House press secretary. People rushed to and fro as if they were late for a meeting or had some pressing engagement to attend. So far, looks like *The West Wing*, I thought—except for the fact that I was in the real transition center of an administration about to assume office rather than working on a Hollywood soundstage.

Arriving in the vice president's outer office, I marveled at how quiet it was in there compared with the activity I had seen in the rest of the building. Other than Debbie Heiden, Cheney's executive assistant (and gatekeeper), and a lone Secret Service agent standing sentry by the door, no other individuals were present.

After a few moments of pleasant small talk with Heiden (could she tell I was really that nervous and was she trying to calm my nerves?), she announced that the VP would see me right away. *Oh, boy. Here goes nothing,* I thought.

I entered the office, and Cheney stood to greet me. He seemed friendly enough, offering me a firm handshake and introducing himself merely as "Dick Cheney." I thought to myself, *What do I call the guy? Mr. Vice President? Mr. Vice President-Elect? Mr. Secretary?* I settled on the middle choice as Cheney ushered me inside and shut the door. To my surprise, no one else was in the room—no Scooter, no Secret Service, nobody.

Interestingly, Cheney's television was tuned to a "Breaking News" prompt on one of the cable television news networks. He settled down in his chair and said he was watching the broadcast and asked me to give him a few minutes. On the screen before us, embattled labor secretary designate Linda Chavez was announcing her intention to withdraw her name from consideration before the United States Senate confirmation process got any further along. *About time,* I thought.

Chavez, an outspoken conservative activist, had brought considerable attention to herself with a disclosure about some of her personal dealings. Needless to say, for an incoming administration that prided itself on restoring dignity and integrity to Washington, Chavez's flap was hardly the beginning anyone had hoped for.

One minute turned into several as Cheney focused on the press conference on TV. I had the distinct impression that he was watching me as much as he was the monitor, but I couldn't tell for certain. Except for the TV, there was silence.

Without warning, the vice president-elect swung around in his chair and asked me what I thought about Chavez announcing the withdrawal of her candidacy. Uh-oh—now what? I replied that I thought it was the proper thing to do since Chavez's media attention was attracting negative attention to the president at a critical time just before his inauguration. It was best for her to go since she was becoming a liability rather than an asset. Cheney replied that my analysis was "about right." (*Thank God!*)

At this point, the vice president ran through my résumé without missing anything I'd done since my graduation from college nearly ten years earlier. This was particularly scary to me since there was no paperwork on Cheney's desk. Not a single sheet. I was pretty impressed that he brought up the fact that he and my old boss, former Ohio Representative John Kasich (R-OH), did not exactly see eye-to-eye on things. From what Don Thibaut, Kasich's former chief of staff, had warned me, this was a polite understatement.

Somehow, the brash Ohio backbencher's vow to reform the Pentagon into a triangle had rubbed the former defense secretary the wrong way. Knowing of Kasich's less than diplomatic approach to those who stood in his way from very personal experience, it didn't surprise me that he had gotten on the wrong side of my potential new boss. What did surprise me was that Cheney was direct and upfront about their relationship and that it had no impact on his decision about me.

About this time, Scooter entered the room without a word, wearing a reassuring smile. Libby had wanted to join our meeting from the beginning, but he had apparently been pulled away momentarily. Without missing a beat, Cheney then outlined his expectations for staff who worked for him. He was hardly the cold, imposing figure I had been told to expect. Without letting too much of my guard down, I finally began to relax.

After discussing his expectations and those of the president, Cheney then asked me if I had any questions to ask of him. *Any questions of him?* I asked how he would expect me to present information to him, assuming that I made it through the selection process. Cheney smiled and told me that he liked receiving a fair amount of background briefings from his staff—particularly written memoranda. He noted that he paid staff not only for what they knew, but for what they thought. I was told not to be afraid to say I didn't know something if he asked—"just don't make a habit of it." All said with a smile.

After about an eternity (really, just about fifteen minutes), Cheney asked the question that I was now prepared to answer without a look of shock on my face. Had I done anything that would embarrass the president and wind up on the front page of the *Washington Post*? "Not a thing," I had replied. With a smile and a handshake, Cheney told me that I would be hearing back from them soon. Was I in?

Scooter walked me down to his office and asked if I had something I needed to tell him, something—*anything*—before a final decision was reached. After hearing the *Washington Post* admonition one last time, Scooter shook my hand and dashed off to another meeting. Was I through? Did I make it? I returned home and immediately checked my answering machine. Nothing.

The next morning, I arrived at Senator-Elect Allen's office where I was serving as his counsel during his transition to office. I had taken a gamble by turning down the senator's offer to become his legislative director (LD) in the hopes that something in the White House would come through. Allen, needing a trusted adviser and friend to help staff his legislative team, had asked me to work for him as his counsel with no strings attached while I went through the interview process on the other end of Pennsylvania Avenue.

Despite the graciousness of Allen's offer, I had taken a calculated risk. The Senator's second choice for the LD position was a smart yet bombastic and opinionated Naval Reserve officer. If I didn't get the job in the VP's office, I would have to work for this guy. That prospect was, at best, frightening. Had I made the right decision?

Every minute of every hour stretched on like an eternity for me as I waited. The phone lines were burning across the Potomac River as I called home at least several times an hour to check my answering machine. Shortly after 10:00 AM, one of Senator Allen's interns stuck his head in my office to say that a Dean McGrath was on the phone for me. Not familiar with the name, I engaged the blinking light, expecting to hear from a prospective applicant to the Senator's legislative team. Word was out on the street that if you wanted to apply for a spot on Allen's legislative team, I was one of the guys to talk to. My phone that morning had been ringing off the hook.

"Hello?" I answered. "Congratulations," came a voice from the other end of the phone. Congratulations for what? Realizing that he hadn't properly identified himself, McGrath quickly explained that he was the VP's deputy chief of staff, and I was being offered a position as the deputy assistant to the vice president for domestic policy. For my entire professional career, from the time I first joined the staff of a member of Congress as a junior legislative correspondent charged with answering the mail, I never dreamed I would have the chance to advise a senator, let alone the vice president of the United States, on domestic policy issues. The brass ring was now being swung slowly in front of me. Grabbing the ring with both hands, I told McGrath I would be honored to join the VP's team. I was in!

Just Another
Manic Monday

22 JANUARY 2001. THE FIRST WORKING DAY IN THE PRESIDENCY of George W. Bush, and I was about to join his team as the deputy assistant to the vice president for domestic policy! I was so excited about my first day that I hadn't slept a wink the night before. This was it: The days of dreaming, planning and praying to join the administration were over. Now it was time to get down to business.

Driving into work, I reflected on the words of advice dispensed by Fox News Channel host (and former President George H. W. Bush speechwriter) Tony Snow as he signed off his broadcast on President Bush's Inauguration Day:

> For those White House newcomers, I offer a few pieces of kindly advice.
>
> First, keep a level head, because if you lose your humility, somebody will return it with compound interest, almost certainly in front of TV cameras.
>
> Second, realize that in Washington you can't take friendship personally. The people kissing up to you now will ignore you when you leave the president's employ.

Third, understand that in this town, the urgent overwhelms the important. Today's crisis is tomorrow's footnote.

Fourth, remember who's in charge. You are a wart on history's nose. The president's the one who counts.

And finally, have fun, because before long, you'll be back where you started, among the tourists looking through the gates at that magical, historical house where Lincoln still walks at night and our highest hopes and dreams reside.

Heading in that morning, I had no idea what to expect, but Snow's advice gave me food for thought. Having spent nearly eight years on Capitol Hill, I knew that it was all about advancing the member of Congress that you worked for rather than your own personal goals. Yet, his advice to have fun sounded fine to me. Perhaps through the stress of working for the vice president, we would find time and ways to have fun.

My pressing thoughts on my job, however, were more immediate than having fun in the vice president's office. I just had no idea what the day would have in store for me. Would we receive an orientation? How long would it be before we had the opportunity to meet with the vice president? Would I have my own office? Headed toward the entrance of the Old Executive Office Building at the corner of 17th Street and Pennsylvania Avenue, I was about to have my questions answered in ways I could never have expected.

8:30 AM. My first step inside the White House Complex found me in a line of fellow staffers who were excitedly chatting with one another as we waited for the Secret Service to access our names and clear us into the building. As I stepped up to the counter, I'm sure my nervousness was palpable as the Secret Service officer behind the desk gave me a giant smile and said, "Welcome to the White House, Mr. Christie."

Donning a white access card with a giant letter "A," with "Appointment" written in smaller letters, I passed through the turnstile. My head reeling, I headed toward the stairwell that would take me to the vice president's office suite two floors above me.

As I climbed the stairwell heading to the second floor, I took in the marble steps, which were well worn and imprinted with the weight of thousands of people who had ascended the stairs in the century before me. While the building had a slightly musty smell to it, there was no mistaking the proximity to power as I glanced at the office doors, continuing up the stairwell. "Office of Cabinet Affairs," proclaimed one door. "Office of White House Counsel," announced another.

Reaching the second floor, I started looking for an office with my name on it. I noticed I was suddenly walking on a checkerboard of black and white marble tiles. What did I say about the looking glass? Just as I was about to make a right turn to head toward the vice president's suite, I received my first glimpse of my new surroundings in the White House, and it was not a pretty sight. The floor was a dirty, filthy, cluttered mess. The chaos before me and all throughout the corridor was unbelievable: Old boxes, papers, and fading pictures of President Clinton and Vice President Gore were everywhere. Broken lamps, saggy furniture, and mismatched chairs and office equipment were scattered about. It looked as if every previous occupant of the second floor of the Old Executive Office Building had emptied their wastebaskets on the floor outside their offices before they left. I couldn't believe it: Is this how people treated the White House before us? It looked more like the set of *Sanford and Son* than the seat of power.

Still perplexed, I headed further down the hallway, and I met my first friendly face and fellow member of the vice president's team. I found David Addington sitting on a faded piece of furniture. "Welcome to

OVP," he said warmly as we shook hands and introduced ourselves. As it turned out, Addington was rejoining the vice president's team as Mr. Cheney's chief legal counsel. Previously, Addington had been with Defense Secretary Cheney at the Pentagon, followed by a stint in private practice. Addington invited me to join him on the "porch" as we awaited our colleagues.

After several minutes of conversation, I promised to return once I found my office and stored my belongings. Heading further down the corridor while navigating around several chairs, couches, and additional trash that had been heaped in the hallway, I entered what I believed to be my office. Inside, I was greeted by three veterans of the Cheney team from the 2000 campaign.

Dan Wilmot, the head of the VP's Advance Team, was the first to say hello. A former Marine, Wilmot was charged with coordinating with the Secret Service to survey and secure the location of venues where the vice president would travel. How many steps from the motorcade to the podium? Dan knew the answer. Evacuation routes in case of trouble? Wilmot had several. I was struck by his happy demeanor and can-do attitude.

Next, I met Elizabeth Kleppe and Mary Kathleen Lang, the vice president's schedulers. They were tasked with sifting through the volumes of requests for the precious time and attention of the vice president. Talking with Elizabeth and Mary as we exchanged our stories as to how we had arrived in the White House, I was struck once again by how friendly all my new colleagues seemed to be. After more than seven years working as a staff member on Capitol Hill, I had braced myself for the airs and egos that I had often encountered from "White House types" during the previous Bush and Clinton administrations.

To be fair, I had found the arrogance and self-importance of staff on the Hill to be as annoying as the politicians themselves. Many confuse working for someone with power with actually having power themselves. I had prepared myself for the worst as I entered the building that morning, convinced I would find staff with egos at least the size of the Old Executive Office Building. Thus far, my fellow colleagues couldn't have been kinder or more down-to-earth.

Continuing my journey down the hall, I finally found Room 286, where I had been directed to report. The brass plate affixed upon the door read: "Office of the Vice President, Domestic Policy." Finally, the right spot! My euphoria was short-lived, however. I was in store for a new treat as I entered my new home away from home.

My office was an absolute disaster. If the litter in the hallway behind me was bad, this was incalculably worse. There were discarded bookcases, desks, and clutter everywhere. For some strange reason, the previous occupants had left numerous copies of the *Webster's Dictionary* both on the floor and upon the bookcases before me. Looking to my left, a small doorway had a simple printed sign with "Christie" upon it.

Ducking inside the doorway, I was confronted by an office workstation with a keyboard beside it. Curiously, the letter "W" was nowhere to be seen on this keyboard. Looking to my right, another desk and chair were set up near a tall window that faced the West Wing of the White House. Once again, the "W" was missing.

Piles of trash lay on the floor before me—along with my computer workstation. I marveled at how anyone could be so utterly destructive, seemingly without concern they would be caught or about the callousness with which they had treated the executive office of the president.

As I would soon discover, I was not the only one who had had the "W" removed from their keyboard or piles of trash and clutter left to greet them. John Gossel, my good friend from the vice president's operations office, had assured me that many other offices in OVP were identical to mine in their appearance as we opened for business that day.

Surprisingly, in the first days following the president's inauguration, former Clinton administration officials maintained in the media that reports of vandalism in the White House were overstated. Nothing more than a few little pranks, the public was told. If these were pranks and practical jokes, I hardly found them amusing as I rummaged through discarded office equipment in the hall for a functioning keyboard, lamp, television, and desk light. It seems the prankster who had occupied the office before me had cheerfully spirited these items away from their proper location.

Pranks and clutter notwithstanding, I was thrilled to be where I was. There was an excitement in the air, and everyone was excited to get down to business—if only we could figure out what that was. One of the things you discover when you work in the White House at the beginning of a new administration is that there is nothing there that has already been set up for you. No files, no memos, no notes, nothing. Apparently, all of the previous administration's work is boxed up, saved on computer disks, and otherwise sent off to the presidential archivist. In reality, that meant that there was no owner's manual on how one is to proceed on their first day in the White House. We would have to make it up on the fly. Despite the fact that our computers were just coming online and I still couldn't find where the paper was for my printer (not that it worked at that point), we were still expected to hit the ground running at full speed.

As it turns out, we wouldn't have to wait long to find out what was expected of us. Shortly following our arrival, we were summoned to a staff meeting convened by Scooter Libby, the vice president's chief of staff (whom I had met during my interviews), to discuss our role in the

White House as members of the vice president's team. I was surprised when I arrived to see Scooter's counterpart, Andrew H. Card Jr., the president's chief of staff, in the room.

Other than the occasional glimpse on television, I had never seen or heard anything about the president's chief of staff. For that matter, I wasn't entirely sure what the chief of staff did on a day-to-day basis. Was he in every meeting with the president? Did he advance the president's agenda or implement his interpretation of what he thought the president meant to achieve? Would he run the White House with an iron fist, or would he be a conciliatory figure? As these thoughts raced through my head, Card broke the silence with a large smile that lit up the room as he stepped forward to welcome us all and express his gratitude for our having joined the president's administration. First he told us about the high honor and privilege Mr. Bush had placed on his service to the country as president of the United States.

On the day of his inauguration, following the swearing-in ceremony and the pomp and circumstance on Capitol Hill, Mr. Bush entered the White House for the first time as president of the United States. Mr. Card was present as President Bush first strode into the freshly repainted Oval Office. Watching as the new president sat behind the H.M.S. *Resolute* desk used by every president of the United States since Rutherford B. Hayes (save Presidents Johnson, Nixon, and Ford), Card marveled as Mr. Bush took in his surroundings in the most powerful office in the world.

Just then, footsteps could be heard coming down the colonnade in the Rose Garden. The door opened up, and a gentleman entered who said, "Mr. President." Silence. The president looked up and said, "Mr. President." Father and son, Presidents Bush 41 and 43. Former President Bush said nothing further, but Card noted that both of their eyes had welled up with tears. For his part, Card told us that tears were streaming down his cheeks as he was overcome by the display of mutual respect from the two presidents. Not only mutual respect for each other, but mutual respect for the presidency of the United States.

At that point, a pin dropping in the vice president's ceremonial office would have sounded like cannon shot. With our attention and eyes riveted upon him, Card stressed how important the vice president's staff would be in working with the president's staff to carry out the goals of the administration and do the business of the American people.

He noted that in order for the White House to function as efficiently as possible, it would be necessary for us to understand both our place and role in the system. Mr. Card described his job as one in which he ensured that the president had sufficient time to carry out his responsibilities. That meant allowing the president time in his schedule to meet with key advisors, time to clear his mind through a workout in the gym, and time to spend with his family in the evening prior to retiring for the night. While we all had many interesting and important ideas/suggestions for the president, Card's test for the president's time was simple: If you needed to see the president, you would see the president. If you wanted to see the president, you would not. Period.

We were further reminded that the White House staff structure was designed to maximize both discipline and efficiency. I learned that there were such things as commissioned officers to the president of the United States, classified in three distinct categories. First, there were assistants to the president. Senior to most of the president's advisors, assistants to the president occupied such jobs as national security advisor, counselor to the president, and senior advisor to the president, and were the official titles of Dr. Condoleezza Rice, Karen Hughes, and Karl Rove, respectively.

Just beneath the assistant level were deputy assistants to the president.

These folks were in charge of important but less senior offices such as the Office of Public Liaison, Office of Intergovernmental Affairs, and the White House Political Office. Deputy assistants also tended to be the officially designated deputies to the assistants themselves. Finally, there were special assistants to the president. Special assistants were the senior "worker bees" who were often charged with implementing the policy directives and assignments given them by assistants and deputy assistants to the president. "Specials" also tended to be the designated deputies to the deputy assistants to the president.

After he explained the various titles and responsibilities of commissioned officers, Card admonished us to follow established White House protocol. Even if we didn't agree with something we were told, if a commissioned officer gives an order to a less senior commissioned officer or other member of the staff, that order should be carried out without complaint or delay.

I further learned that the vice president only had two commissioned officers on his staff: Scooter had the three titles of assistant to the president, chief of staff to the vice president, and national security advisor to the vice president, and Mary Matalin was both assistant to the president and counselor to the vice president. As the Constitution spelled out that the vice president's main duty was to preside over the United States Senate, he did not have the authority to dispense commissions—only the president had such power. Therefore, my title as deputy assistant to the vice president for domestic policy meant that in the VP's organizational chart, I was at a relatively senior level, but I did not carry either the rank or the authority of a commissioned officer to the president.

Finally, Card told us not to strive for presidential commissions or seek to make a career in the White House for a lengthy period of time. As there were barely one hundred commissions available, Card stressed that most who sought such an appointment would never get one. Moreover, we were warned not to get too comfortable or complacent— most staff in the White House served for a period of eighteen months or less. Mr. Card said that he didn't expect to serve beyond that point, himself. Instead, we were challenged to work hard, do the work of the American people, and then leave government service to allow others the rare opportunity and privilege to serve.

As we gave Card a round of applause following his intimidating yet inspirational remarks, I was moved at how personal and almost emotional Card had become when discussing the honor and privilege of public service in the White House. I think the gravity of his remarks impacted us all. As the president had spoken eloquently during the campaign that he would bring a different tone and discipline to the White House, Andy Card had given us our first indication that the reverence and respect with which the 43rd president of the United States viewed his job and ours were not mere campaign rhetoric. Bush had meant what he had said about restoring honor and dignity to the People's House.

As intrigued as I was about the thoughts Andy Card expressed regarding our mission in the vice president's office, I was still eager to hear from Mr. Cheney himself. Days later, I learned that we would all meet with the vice president in his ceremonial office for a surprise birthday party being thrown by his wife and daughters. While Cheney might not have known he would be meeting with us, we were all eager as a staff to be in the same room with him.

30 January 2001. The vice president's ceremonial office is centrally located on the second floor of the Old Executive Office Building. Within the past few decades, the ceremonial office has been fully restored to resemble its appearance from the days when it was used as the Navy Secretary's Office back in the day that the OEOB contained

the Navy, State, and War Departments. Maverick Theodore Roosevelt himself had set up camp here in another era, prior to his Rough Riding days and tenure as president of the United States.

This has been both the ceremonial and working home of every vice president since 1960—with a roster that includes everyone from Lyndon Baines Johnson to Richard Bruce Cheney (save Hubert Humphrey). Upon entering the room from the main entrance, one is greeted by creaky hardwood floors that are buffed and polished to perfection. Overhead, there are chandelier replicas of 1900 gasoliers, which were removed from the original furnishings and never recovered. Standing guard to the right is an old wooden desk that was first manned by Theodore Roosevelt and subsequently utilized by Presidents Taft, Wilson, Harding, Coolidge, Hoover, and Eisenhower. Opening the middle drawer of the desk, previous vice presidents have added their names and signatures to history; I couldn't help but notice that Al Gore had signed his name not once, but twice.

Speaking of Gore, to the far end of the room was a door from which the former vice president had entered just weeks before to announce to the world that he had conceded the election to then-Governor Bush. In short, there was a piece of history around every corner of the room.

It seemed only fitting that Vice President Cheney would meet with his entire staff for the first time in a room filled with such historical significance. I didn't have any idea what to expect when Mr. Cheney addressed us, but I sensed that his presentation would lend an important sense of purpose and direction to us all.

These and other questions were pushed aside when the vice president strode into the room—much to his "surprise" as we called out our birthday greetings. As if on cue, I noticed that those staff who were seated rose as one as soon as Cheney was visible. I later learned that it was proper to rise when either the vice president or the president entered a room.

Like the rest of my colleagues, I took a moment to assess and take stock of our new boss.

On this his sixtieth birthday, Mr. Cheney had a reputation and résumé that long preceded his arrival that day. Slightly balding, with grayish hair, the vice president looked every bit the part of the self-assured executive that he was. He was the youngest chief of staff to the president of the United States under President Ford at the ripe age of thirty-four, a five-term congressman from Wyoming, secretary of defense under President George H.W. Bush, and chief executive officer of the Halliburton Corporation in Houston, Texas. Cheney was considered the consummate dealmaker and insider, but I wondered how he would treat all of us.

As we cheered and began to slice up the rather large cake that was set before us (no shy wallflowers in this group!), the VP walked straight to the middle of the room and took centerstage. After thanking us for our singing and wishing him a happy birthday, he became serious for a moment as he reflected upon our role as members of his staff.

First, he thanked us for all of the hard work we had put in to get to this point and expressed the fact that he looked forward to working with all of us in the days to come. In direct and succinct commentary, he reiterated what he said during my interview with him. He would be very interested to know not just what we knew, but what we were thinking, as this would allow him the best opportunity to present his own counsel to the president.

As the vice president articulated his expectations of us, I couldn't help but reflect on a few things. First, Mr. Cheney seemed genuinely touched that nearly his entire staff had joined his immediate family to sing "Happy Birthday" and present him with a gift that remains on his wall in his West Wing office to this day: a large map depicting the route one of his relatives had taken as a captain in the Union Army during the Civil War.

This second meeting with Cheney failed yet again to reveal the cold, gruff, mean person I had prepared myself to expect. The Cheney before us was warm, funny, and apparently embarrassed by all the fuss surrounding his birthday. The look of genuine love and affection that he shone upon his wife, Lynne Vincent Cheney, was clear for all to see. I'm always careful about making snap judgments, but at this point Dick Cheney seemed to be a rather nice guy. I was hoping this would continue to be the case over the long run.

Before I could reflect upon Cheney's words or my initial impressions of him at any length, the back door to the ceremonial office was abruptly opened. Looking to my left, I noticed that large numbers of the White House press corps had begun streaming into the room. What was going on? Almost on cue, the president of the United States strode through another door to wish his seemingly astonished vice president a happy birthday. While Cheney had been warm and amiable during his discussion with the staff, there was a marked change in his demeanor when the press entered the room. I had never met a politician who shied away from a camera lens or a microphone stand, but Dick Cheney seemed to be the exception to that rule. Despite many entreaties by the press for either the president or the VP to say something, the press was quickly herded out of the room.

Immediately upon their departure, the atmosphere lightened in the room, and the president began to dig into the birthday cake with gusto. One piece wasn't enough for Bush, as he picked up a second immediately after he devoured the first—all with a big smile on his face.

If the electricity among the staff with the vice president being in the room was strong, it nearly sizzled with both Bush and Cheney standing before the staff eating birthday cake. Many of us just openly gawked at the two men and Mrs. Cheney as they amiably conversed just feet in front of us. Sadly, the party was over nearly as quickly as it started, and the president and the VP soon left to return to work. Excited and inspired by my encounter with two of the most powerful men in the world, I returned to my office to get down to business.

The Perceived Power Struggle: President v. Vice President

AFTER GOVERNOR BUSH SELECTED THE FORMER WYOMING congressman and secretary of defense to spearhead the search for a viable vice presidential candidate, many in the media and around Washington D.C. assumed that Cheney would pick a telegenic, street-savvy politician who would deliver key electoral college votes come November. Needless to say, the entire political establishment was shocked when the governor later announced that Dick Cheney himself would join the ticket. Dick Cheney? Wasn't he the elderly, balding guy—a staunch ultraconservative with a history of heart trouble? Didn't Wyoming only have two electoral votes? Anyone having heard Cheney speak before would hardly put him in the same charismatic league as a Bill Clinton or Bob Dole. The media circus surrounding Cheney's selection went into overdrive and thus began in earnest the media's depiction of George W. Bush as an amiable Texas lightweight who had chosen his father's defense secretary to show Junior the ways of Washington and the world. Did Bush even choose Cheney, or was he just doing what he was told?

Saturday Night Live capitalized on this, running skits in which the governor was depicted as a churlish little boy who was told how to act and behave by an evil and manipulative Dick Cheney. Mainstream media soon joined in with stories that made no attempt to hide their disdain for Bush's perceived lack of intellect and strongly insinuated that Cheney was the puppet master behind the scenes pulling all the strings of the candidate. Following the election and the Florida recount, Cheney mania reached new heights as the administration settled into office. Would Cheney serve as the *real* president?

The *New York Times*'s coverage of Cheney in the early days of the administration was typical of the garbage we found in the newspaper each day. Just the second week into the administration, I found the following headline blaring at me from the front page: "Cheney Assembles Formidable Team." Well, our folks were pretty talented, but formidable? A bit melodramatic, perhaps. The article continued:

> Vice President Dick Cheney is assembling a powerful parallel White House staff, including a mini National Security Council and domestic policy staff, to support his formidable role in shaping the Bush agenda and brokering it on Capitol Hill. . . . Mr. Cheney's staff is closely integrated with President Bush's White House team and so far numbers about 50 people, including schedulers, speechwriters and secretaries—about half of what Vice President Al Gore's staff was at its peak—but it is growing. (*New York Times*, 3 February 2001)

For one, the last thing the vice president or any of us wanted to do was assemble a powerful and parallel White House staff. Our marching orders had already been articulated by White House Chief of Staff Andy Card and Cheney himself: Support the president and his team in any way we could. For Cheney, this task was made easier by the fact that he held no presidential ambitions himself. Arguably, the United States has not seen a vice president without presidential ambitions since 1929, when President Herbert Hoover chose sixty-nine-year-old Charles Curtis to be his running mate. Harboring no desire to sit in the Oval Office in his own administration allowed Cheney to focus exclusively on performing tasks given by the president for him to perform.

Early in the administration, the vice president was tasked by the president with chairing a Budget Review Group to resolve arguments between cabinet secretaries and White House Budget Director Mitch Daniels once Daniels submitted his FY 2002 budget to the president just weeks away. Given that one of my assignments was to brief the VP on budget, tax, and entitlement issues, I knew my plate would be full here. Cabinet secretaries would undoubtedly balk at any reductions in spending, and our conservative allies on Capitol Hill would insist that the president submit a budget to reflect conservative desires to curb discretionary spending. I knew that a potential storm was ahead, and I would have to be on top of my facts and figures.

The president had also asked the VP to convene an energy task force that would examine the problems facing America and issue a detailed report on how to fix them. Further still, the VP would be an important proponent overall of the president's fledgling agenda on Capitol Hill. As the former whip of the Republican Caucus during his stint on the Hill, Cheney would be able to balance the myriad concerns facing members of Congress while reminding them of the importance of passing the president's initiatives.

Given Cheney's background as secretary of defense, the president also relied heavily on his vice president's counsel on matters pertaining to foreign affairs and national security. Cheney was well versed in both the worlds of diplomacy and war. In the first Bush administration, he had directed Operation Just Cause in Panama and Operation Desert Storm in the Middle East. During his stint as secretary of defense, Cheney also worked with leaders around the world to move America and her allies toward a new day where the threat of the Cold War had finally ended.

The current secretary of defense, Donald H. Rumsfeld, was an old Cheney ally and in fact was Cheney's boss when Cheney served as Rumsfeld's deputy chief of staff in the Ford White House. Their strong rapport would undoubtedly only enhance the stream of information headed to the president.

Finally, the vice president was an early and frequent spokesman for the Bush administration in our opening days. Communications Director Mary Matalin and her press secretary, Juleanna Glover Weiss, were constantly fielding requests to have Cheney make the rounds on the Sunday talk shows and sit for countless interviews for print and radio. In short, our staff was swamped with work.

Behind this backdrop of Cheney conspiracy theorists smugly intoning that the VP was actually running the world, I settled down in my office in the Old Executive Office Building to figure out how to serve the man widely believed to be the most powerful vice president in the history of the United States. While I had the feeling that the White House staff didn't necessarily believe the media hype surrounding the influence of the vice president, I had the sense they weren't thrilled with the media's persistent coverage of Cheney, either. From day one, I had the impression that the president and his team wanted to turn the focus away from eight years of the Clinton administration—particularly the last-minute pardons and vandalism left by the departing staff—to begin a new era with the Bush administration. Needless to say, media accounts glorifying the vice president and his power didn't quite seem to fit in with the image of President Bush being a strong, decisive leader who was firmly in charge.

In our opening days in office, I was pleased to participate in a newspaper interview with the *Washington Post* in which they asked key members of the vice president's staff to describe their roles and responsibilities. The *Post* was further interested to know how closely we were integrated with the president's staff. Mary Matalin, the renowned Republican strategist turned counselor to the vice president, had asked that I field questions from Dana Milbank, a veteran reporter of the *Washington Post*, to discuss how the VP's domestic policy staff would work with the president's. I was honored by Matalin's request, and I set out to tell one and all how we were seamlessly integrated and joined at the hip to fulfill the president's domestic agenda.

While I thought the questions posed by Milbank were relatively straightforward, I would soon discover the hard way how reporters in Washington D.C. have the unique ability to take your remarks and spin them out of context, making you look foolish or worse. While I thought I had accurately portrayed the role of our staff vis-à-vis the president's staff as being nothing more than supplemental and supportive, my printed remarks didn't quite come out that way. Suffice it to say that when the article was published that weekend, my remarks essentially set off a stink bomb in the West Wing with the president's staff, as well as with a noted conservative commentator.

On 3 February 2001, the *Washington Post* ran an article entitled "For Number Two the Future Is Now: Cheney Has Historically Broad Agenda." In the typically dramatic prose of the time, the *Post* noted that "Cheney, a veteran Washington hand, has been given what White House officials say is unprecedented power within the White House." The article further observed that "[Cheney] has so far integrated the vice presidential staff seamlessly with the presidential staff, allowing the White House to speak with a unified voice as it deals with

Congress and the public." Exactly the message we were looking to convey. Close to the end of the article, my quotation appeared.

While I had told Mr. Milbank that my friends in previous administrations had felt that the White House staff had run the show with no exceptions, I had noted that this administration differed in that Vice President Cheney's staff had the ability to sit side by side with the president's staff. At the end of the day, however, I told Milbank we were there to help the president and his team however, whenever, and wherever possible.

But my remarks to Mr. Milbank didn't quite make it into print as I had hoped. Instead, my heart sank when I opened the paper and found the following:

[Cheney's deputy domestic policy advisor] Ron Christie, a former aide to John R. Kasich (R-Ohio) works on entitlement policy with his old friend, John Bridgeland, a Bush policy aide. "The sense I get talking to my friends who worked in past administrations, they really felt the White House ran the show," Christie said. But this time, he added, "It's equal footing."

Lovely. For all the lengths I had gone to paint the VP and his staff as strong supporters of the president and his staff, it looked to the world as if I felt we were equal partners—almost a co-presidency. Undoubtedly, this was just the type of image the press had wanted to impress upon a public that was still somewhat wary of Bush's leadership skills and rather convinced his vice president was running the show. But in spite of my misgivings, I reasoned that things might not be as bad as they seemed.

My fear deepened the following day, however, when I tuned in to the talk show *Fox News Sunday* to catch the latest political buzz. During a roundtable with the Fox News Channel's political commentators, veteran conservative journalist (and former chief of staff to Vice President Quayle) William Kristol weighed in on my comments made in the *Washington Post* article the day before! I was shocked to listen to Kristol opine that some Cheney aide thought that the VP's staff and the president's were essentially equal. I tried to console myself with the fact that Kristol didn't mention me by name on national television. Perhaps I was overreacting, and my comments wouldn't cause a stir with the brass over in the West Wing.

If only I would be that lucky. As the two members of the vice president's team who were also members of the president's staff, Mary Matalin and Scooter Libby attended the president's senior staff meeting every morning. During these meetings, headlines from over the night and over the weekend are often discussed. As fate would have it, Matalin told me later that morning that my comments had been discussed at senior staff—and they weren't a hit. Apparently Andy Card himself had weighed in personally with his thoughts of my "we're all equal" comments. With a smile on her face, Matalin suggested that I might want to keep a low profile and my thoughts about the role of the vice president to myself for a while.

This wasn't the opening impression I had wanted to leave with the president's staff, but neither Matalin nor Libby seemed too concerned about my media transgression. Perhaps they knew that I had bigger concerns as I sought to get up to speed on my issues, prepare my initial briefing memos for the vice president, and await our first policy briefing.

The Domestic
Policy Machine

EARLY IN OUR TENURE, WE WERE TOLD BOTH BY SCOOTER AND Deputy Chief of Staff Dean McGrath that the vice president had a voracious appetite for information. While we would soon sit down with the VP for weekly face-to-face policy briefings, Cheney also expected us to prepare written memoranda for him on policy matters within our respective issue areas. Given my background as the former legislative director for the House Budget Committee chairman, I was initially tasked with advising the vice president on budget, tax, and entitlement issues such as Social Security and Medicare reform. My policy portfolio also included healthcare, agriculture, and the environment, just to name a few. Given the small size of our initial domestic policy staff (four), we faced a daunting task in trying to cover our policy issues, connect with our counterparts on the president's staff, and accurately advise the vice president on the latest developments.

We immediately plugged into the White House policy apparatus to remain abreast of current developments. As one who works better face to face rather than over the telephone, I spent the first several weeks walking throughout the White House complex introducing myself to my counterparts on the president's domestic policy team. As I would discover, my initial outreach efforts to make inroads with my colleagues on the president's staff proved extremely beneficial over time.

First, I was invited to join the daily Domestic Policy Council (DPC) briefings conducted by Margaret Spellings, the president's chief domestic policy advisor (currently serving as the secretary of education) and John Bridgeland, her deputy. These meetings, held daily at 8:30 AM in a cramped conference room within the Old Executive Office Building, allowed the president's domestic policy advisors to convene on a daily basis, swap notes with their colleagues, and receive direction on areas in which the president and/or his senior staff required additional information. Most important, they allowed all of us to bond with each other, vent our frustrations, and learn how to navigate the tricky currents of White House staff life together.

Spellings was a big hit with the domestic policy staff from day one. Tall, with short blond hair and small, no-nonsense glasses, Spellings is blessed with a sense of humor that would make a professional comedian proud. Margaret was quite at home cracking jokes and poking fun at herself and the staff in her slow Texas drawl. Nothing and no one escaped her attention, and she soon labeled most of us with a nickname or term of affection.

Beneath the wit and the barbs, however, Margaret was all business: a task-oriented boss who did not accept staff who were either unprepared or unable to answer the myriad questions she would fire off as she sought to shape the president's initial policy initiatives. Those found unprepared or needing extra assistance from her were told to "stay after class," an invitation which could lead to a private tongue-lashing. "Staying after class" was a field trip I wanted to avoid at all costs, so I remained on guard for any questions about what the vice president might be saying or doing.

Participating in the DPC meetings every morning provided me with real-time intelligence about what the president and his senior staff were thinking about how he would unveil his initial domestic policy initiatives. Equally important, the president's team got to know me and the issues I was covering for the VP. I carried this information back to Cesar Conda, my boss and assistant to the vice president for domestic policy—Cheney's top domestic policy advisor. A native Virginian, Cesar was oftentimes quiet and unassuming. At the same time, Cesar had a quick sense of humor, and we hit it off instantly. Every morning, I stuck my head in his door following the DPC meetings and filled him in. We reviewed what the president's people were focusing on and discussed what information or materials we thought the vice president would be interested in reviewing.

As the vice president settled into his massive duties and responsibilities, he started scheduling briefings with his staff to discuss domestic policy issues. When our time to meet was upon us, I was excited to formally sit down with our boss and get down to business. As Cesar and I walked to our first briefing, we were also joined by Nina Shokraii Rees, my fellow deputy domestic policy advisor. Originally from Iran, Rees immigrated to the United States as a young girl and had spent much of her professional career as an expert in education policy. Given the emphasis of education reform during the presidential campaign, Nina was already hard at work with her White House counterparts putting the final pieces of the president's new plan together. (Today, Nina is the assistant deputy secretary for innovation and improvement at the Department of Education.)

Andrew Lundquist, the former staff director of the Senate Energy and Natural Resources Committee, also joined us. As the president had ordered the VP to convene an energy task force and make recommendations later that spring, Lundquist would be heavily involved in the decision-making process. Our team was rounded out by our Deputy Chief of Staff Dean McGrath, Scooter Libby, and Mary Matalin.

While the vice president maintains a ceremonial office in the Old Executive Office Building, his personal office is located on the first floor of the West Wing, just steps away from the Oval Office itself. This is the office where Cheney meets with foreign dignitaries, cabinet secretaries, and members of his personal staff. As we settled into our routine, we would generally brief the vice president for thirty to forty-five minutes every Tuesday. Individually, we would also join the vice president for meetings with business leaders, economists, and others, provided the subject matter was within our issue area.

With this being my first briefing, however, I wanted to soak in all the details. Vice President Cheney's office is a rather spacious affair on the first floor of the West Wing of the White House, just next door to White House Chief of Staff Andy Card. Large bay windows provide strong natural light on one side of the room and are bracketed by two portraits of former vice presidents: Thomas Jefferson and John Quincy Adams. Deep blue carpet covers the floor and matches the dark blue couch where guests are invited to sit. The VP's large wooden desk is framed by the flags of the United States and Wyoming on the left and the vice presidential flag of office and the black POW/MIA (Prisoner of War/Missing in Action) flag on the right. Soon, the wall behind the desk would be adorned with the large map given to Cheney at his surprise party.

We settled into the vice president's seating area in a horseshoe pattern around him. I was on the couch facing the fireplace, with Nina Rees to my left and Scooter sitting on a chair immediately to my right. The vice president was seated on Scooter's left-hand side facing the door, in a tall white chair with gold and light blue stripes. Cesar sat in a smaller wooden chair directly across from the VP, while Andrew Lundquist and Mary Matalin completed the horseshoe pattern to Cesar's right.

With little fanfare, the vice president kicked off our meeting by looking to Cesar and saying with a smile, "Okay, what have we got, Cesar?" Cesar began by reviewing the active tax cut options that were being readied for President Bush's review.

During the campaign, Bush had promised to stimulate the economy, which had become sluggish in the later years of the Clinton administration. On 31 January 2001, the Commerce Department had downgraded the Fourth Quarter 2000 Gross Domestic Product (GDP) growth estimates from 2.2 percent to an anemic 1.4 percent. Also that month, in testimony before the Senate Budget Committee, Alan Greenspan, chairman of the Federal Reserve Bank Board of Governors, had noted that economic growth in the United States was "probably very close to zero." To combat these dismal economic forecasts, Bush sought to work with the Congress to pass legislation that would provide across-the-board reductions in the marginal tax rates paid by working Americans.

An economist by training, Conda also knew that providing a strong stimulus to the economy was high on the vice president's radar screen—lest America slide into a recession that would have far-reaching consequences. Cesar discussed the latest thinking among then Director of the White House Economic Council Larry Lindsey, Secretary of Treasury Paul O'Neill, and Commerce Secretary Don Evans, along with others. Before I knew it, Conda turned to me and said, "Ron will now give you a quick update on the budget review process." I was on!

For all of my recollections of conversations I've had with people over the years, I can honestly say that I have no vivid recollection as to what my first words to Vice President Cheney were in my official capacity. None at all. I do recall my heart beating so loudly that I was convinced everyone in the room could hear it. I also remember sitting on one of my hands so that neither the VP nor my colleagues could see it shaking. But as to my actual words in the briefing? I just think my nerves got the better of me.

After what felt like an eternity (in reality no longer than one minute), I was finished saying whatever it was that I had to say. For his part, Cheney smiled at me, nodded his head, and then moved on to the next briefer. I had made it through unscathed. Not an insignificant accomplishment given the mystique and the reputation the VP had for not suffering fools lightly. Not that I thought I was a fool—just looking for validation that my presentation of the issues didn't leave Cheney totally baffled.

As would prove to be the case during our domestic policy discussions and other meetings, Cheney was comfortable letting his staff brief without interjecting and weighing in unless it was necessary for him to correct something, pose a question, or offer an observation. Over time, I realized that the best briefing or meeting to be had with the VP was one in which he didn't pose any questions. Questions from him often led to a grilling where you knew he possessed more expertise on the topic than you did. Perhaps this was his way of silently pushing us to be as well prepared as we could before visiting with him. Regardless, I soon adopted a "Cheney-esque" style that drove my colleagues around the White House complex crazy: I would arrive at meetings, sit silently, and monitor the conversation, only offering my thoughts where necessary. Oftentimes, I suspected people of speaking to hear themselves speak in meetings, and I wanted nothing to do with that type of attention-getting behavior. Instead, I wanted to be respected to the extent that if I was actually weighing in on a discussion, people would sit up and take notice of my comments since I didn't offer them indiscriminately.

The Real Dick Cheney

THE DICK CHENEY TO WHOM WE BECAME ACCUSTOMED WAS the same one we had initially encountered during our personal interviews—nice, subdued, talkative, but almost a touch on the shy side. Media accounts of the evil genius or the conniving puppet master orchestrating all the president's moves were just not an accurate portrayal of the man we knew. Perhaps only his family and closest friends know the real Dick Cheney away from the public eye, but we would come to admire and become fiercely loyal to the man who was often derided in the press because of the way he relied on and showed respect toward his staff.

As winter gave way to spring, I found my personal involvement with the vice president's policy apparatus grew more and more by the day. I started digging in and producing numerous policy memoranda for the vice president's review. Al Gore's elusive Medicare "lockbox"? I had one in. Tax cuts progress on the president's budget? Social Security reform? I kept the paper trail from my office to the VP's burning. As my confidence grew in writing, Cesar encouraged me to be present with the vice president for meetings in his office that pertained to my public policy subject areas as often as possible.

This was a rather gracious step, as senior managers on Capitol Hill and in the White House had been known to jealously guard their time with the principal. Not so with Cesar. Given his vast responsibilities to manage our entire staff as well as formulate tax policy with his counterparts at the National Economic Council, Cesar was more than willing to share some of the wealth of VP face time. Not wishing to kick a gift horse in the mouth, I jumped at the opportunity to slowly build up my own professional and personal rapport with Mr. Cheney.

If my memory serves me correctly, the first opportunity I had to sit in on a meeting with the vice president took place in late February 2001. Daniel Goldin, the current (but soon to be outgoing) administrator of NASA, had wanted to pay the VP a courtesy call. Goldin had been the longest serving administrator of the space agency, having started back during the administration of George H.W. Bush. Goldin apparently had strong ties to former Vice President Gore and (according to my sources at NASA) was looking to use his meeting with Cheney as an opportunity to hold on to his job. The opportunity to observe the face-to-face discussion was one which excited me.

Prior to the meeting, I had already tipped off the VP that Goldin was looking to gauge Cheney's general interest in the space program. I had also been made aware that Goldin might seek to ascertain the VP's level of interest in the International Space Station (ISS) as well as Cheney's thoughts regarding Russian involvement in the ISS. What I didn't tell him was that a senior member of his staff had alerted me in advance that Goldin wanted to stay in his position, which was why he wanted to have a face-to-face briefing with the VP. My thought at the time was that this was something I didn't need to get involved in, and the VP could certainly handle that if it arose.

At the designated time, I escorted Administrator Goldin over to the

VP's West Wing office. After a few moments, the VP's heavy outer door swung open, and we were invited to enter. When meeting with visitors, the vice president sits in his customary tall chair right beside the working fireplace. Guests are invited to sit in an identical chair to Cheney's left. Any additional visitors and/or staff are encouraged to sit on the couch directly facing the fireplace to the VP's left side. The VP started the meeting by thanking Goldin for his long tenure at NASA. True to form, Goldin had inquired about the VP's interest in the space program in general and the International Space Station in particular. As would prove the case during my tenure in the VP's office, Cheney was extremely well prepared and well versed in the subject matter—discussing complex items at length that I had never covered in my background briefings or memos.

Sitting in the meeting that day was somewhat awkward for me as the elephant surveyed everyone from the middle of the room. It was apparent that my intel was correct: Goldin clearly wanted to stay at the helm of the space agency; however, Cheney never opened the door to such a possibility during our meeting, instead focusing on the substantive issues being discussed.

Thankfully, our meeting with Goldin was short, and I was soon escorting him from the West Wing. As I was a huge space buff and a personal fan of Dan Goldin, our walk outside was not an entirely pleasurable one. For Goldin, I'm sure the meeting clearly hadn't ended in the manner he had hoped, an impression a senior NASA official later confidentially confirmed. For me, I felt uncomfortable watching someone who had perhaps just realized that the sands had emptied through the hourglass, his time expired. Shaking hands and walking back, I was glad this meeting had come to an end.

Several observations came to mind as I reviewed our meeting. First,

I was impressed with how conversational and "normal" the vice president had been with his guest. I've sat in on countless meetings with congressmen and senators over the years, and many adopt a regal tone and bearing that is both arrogant and amusing at the same time. Not so with the VP. While very quiet and unassuming in his demeanor, Cheney is rather demonstrative with his hands as he engages in conversation. Knowledgeable without being a know-it-all, Cheney didn't fill the room with idle chitchat and banter; he just said what needed to be said and left it at that.

Ultimately, Goldin remained at NASA for several more months. He even requested a meeting with the VP later that year that I attended in which he personally told Cheney about his plans to move along. Similar to the first meeting, the VP was gracious and complimentary of Goldin's service. This time, Goldin was at ease and clearly at peace with his decision to depart the administration.

Another story that comes to mind occurred during the spring of 2001 when the vice president and I had the opportunity to sit down with world-renowned historian Stephen Ambrose. Ambrose, best known for his riveting accounts of American men and women on the battlefield during World War II, had requested the opportunity to meet with the VP regarding the restoration of the Missouri River. As had become the case in our office, Cesar passed on the opportunity to staff the meeting and instead asked me to sit in with the VP and Ambrose.

Prior to the meeting, the VP had asked me to check out the history surrounding efforts to manage the Missouri River. Cheney believed that the issue had been controversial during his tenure in Congress, and he wanted me to be able to provide him with a briefing on the issues presented as well as what Mr. Ambrose might want from him. The vice president's memory was right on target as usual: In advance of activity by the Army Corps of

Engineers regarding plans to dam the river in Montana and the Dakotas, several governors had written the president to express their concern that this would have disastrous effects on areas farther downstream. I reported back these facts, along with Mr. Ambrose's desire to restore the Missouri River to resemble its appearance in time to celebrate the bicentennial of Lewis and Clark's expedition. I wasn't sure if that was possible, but I thought the discussion would be interesting nonetheless.

I arrived at our meeting eager to meet Mr. Ambrose; I was so anxious, in fact, that I had left behind one of his books that I had brought to the office for him to autograph. No matter. The vice president was clearly happy to see Ambrose, and they spent the first several minutes talking about fishing (the VP is an avid fly fisherman) and the outdoors. When talk turned to business, Ambrose told the VP that the plan to dam the Missouri River was not controversial and that it was supported in several states downstream. What? This was entirely incorrect, and I wondered if Ambrose was intentionally misleading the vice president, assuming we would believe anything he said outright.

As the meeting progressed, I listened with a certain degree of angst as Ambrose made his case. The last straw for me was when Ambrose claimed that the plan to dam the Missouri River was widely supported in the State of Missouri itself. Widely supported? The Missouri House of Representatives had just recently voted unanimously to denounce the plan!

During all of this, Cheney was attentive and observant to both his guest and to his fidgeting deputy domestic policy advisor who could hardly contain himself. In meetings with the vice president in which guests other than his staff are present, we quickly learned that it was the best course of action not to interject unless instructed to do so by the VP. In the Ambrose meeting, I bit my tongue several times as I wanted to challenge the historian on his recitation of the facts.

As I was stewing in my seat listening to the conversation between the two of them, without warning Cheney looked over to me and asked if I had any questions I wanted to ask Mr. Ambrose. Was that a twinkle in his eye or just my imagination? Apparently given the green light, I immediately challenged Mr. Ambrose to explain how residents of Missouri were supportive of the Army Corps' plan when the entire Missouri House of Representatives had voted 138-0 to denounce plans for federal involvement. Further, I asked why Missouri Governor Bob Holden had joined several other governors in voicing their opposition via a letter to President Bush.

As soon as I posed my questions, a cold front blew into the first floor of the West Wing and settled in the VP's office. Clearly, Mr. Ambrose was used to doing the asking rather than the answering of questions and was unused to anyone challenging his veracity. Too bad, I thought.

Given that it is such a rare honor to be able to discuss issues with the vice president in the first place, I couldn't believe what I had just done. Clearly, my ability to contain my temper in the face of inaccurate representations needed some work. As a visibly angry Ambrose began to rebut my assertions, it was clear to me that the vice president had heard all that he needed to hear.

Always polite and engaging, Cheney thanked his guest for stopping by to see him. As for me, I was merely terrified. Did I cross a line? Was the VP ticked off that I had essentially called one of the most prominent historians in America a liar to his face? As was his custom, Cheney kept his thoughts to himself.

Rather than beat myself up over the matter, I left the meeting with Ambrose and the VP and buried myself in other issues, pretty much blocking the meeting out of my mind. I was surprised several days later when I received word that the vice president wanted me to draft a letter to send to Mr. Ambrose in which the VP would express his inability to advocate Ambrose's plan to President Bush.

Wow! Did my interjection help sway Cheney's opinion? Did he know what Ambrose was up to all along? He never told me and I never asked, but I felt that he had trusted and acted upon my interjection in our meeting that day. To me, this was the best form of praise I could have received. From that day forward, I felt as though the vice president of the United States had placed sufficient trust and confidence in my abilities that he was comfortable allowing me to take a more active role in my meetings with him.

If the Ambrose meeting illustrated how tense our meetings could be with folks, another we had with the Wyoming Wool Growers Association proved how relaxed they could be. Perhaps the ten years Cheney served in the House of Representatives as the lone representative from Wyoming had given him an appreciation of how important it was to hear directly from his constituency. While the entire country was now his elected constituency rather than just the approximately 500,000 from the Cowboy State, the vice president really seemed to enjoy meeting with people outside the Washington K Street crowd who so often sought an audience with him.

Late in the spring of 2001, representatives from the Wool Growers made their way to the White House to visit with their "local boy done good" in Washington. Like the VP, I genuinely enjoyed meeting with people from outside the Beltway. After nearly eight years on Capitol Hill as a legislative aide, I found that people whose lives do not revolve around either the federal budget or the legislative cycle on Capitol Hill often bring a refreshing viewpoint to the table when discussing issues.

On May 11, I met with six members of the Wool Growers in the historic conference room adjacent to the Oval Office, and together we waited for Mr. Cheney to arrive. The Roosevelt Room was named by President Nixon in 1969 to commemorate the contributions of Theodore and Franklin Roosevelt to the construction and expansion of the West Wing of the White House. The room was the original site of the president's office in 1902 before the West Wing renovations were completed seven years later. President Franklin Delano Roosevelt's staff originally called the room the "Fish Room" as FDR brought in an aquarium and filled the room with bounty he had caught from the sea. The Fish Room tradition continued in the Kennedy administration, as JFK mounted a marlin on the wall that he had caught off the coast of Acapulco, Mexico. Today the room is used as the conference room for the president, vice president, and senior members of the White House staff.

As we waited, we all took in the decorations and memorabilia on the walls around us. On the eastern end of the room, Theodore Roosevelt peered down at us from a portrait in which he sat astride a rearing horse. Just beneath the portrait stood the Congressional Medal of Honor Roosevelt had been posthumously awarded in 2001 for his bravery in leading the Rough Riders in the Battle of San Juan Hill nearly a century ago. Located nearby was a simple gold coin encased in glass on the mantelpiece beneath the portrait that contained the Nobel Peace Prize Teddy Roosevelt had been awarded for negotiating the end of the war between Japan and Russia in 1905.

On the southern wall, the American flag was bracketed by flags from each branch of the uniformed armed forces. Streamers at the top of each flag denoted important battles and conflicts that branch of the military had participated in. Finally, a portrait of FDR adorned the western wall that portrayed a beaming and serene creator of the New Deal.

Following our brief tour around the room, I arrayed the group around the table, with three Wool Growers on either side of the table, a space for

Cheney at the head, and a chair to his right for me. The doorknob turned behind us, and I immediately stood up, the others following my lead. The vice president entered the room with a large smile on his face, and he circled the table to greet each one of his visitors. Even with the VP within the West Wing of the White House, I couldn't help but notice the agents from the United States Secret Service had surveyed the room and remained outside of the room as they shut the door behind us.

As we settled down to business, the VP was visibly animated talking about his beloved Wyoming. As was usually the case, the visitors came bearing gifts.

First, the group presented Cheney with a set of handmade fishing lures. Considering his passion for fishing, it's no surprise that the box hadn't been in his hands for more than a few seconds before he was removing the rubber band around the container to check out the lures inside. It was clear that this gift meant more to him than many he had received. As the VP marveled at the lures before him, one of the Wool Growers slid the vice president's next gift down the table for his review. A white, furry object came sliding past me down the table.

I glanced over at the VP to see if it looked like he knew what this thing was. His expression of surprise and amusement said that he was as bewildered as I was. The VP, however, was as gracious as always and thanked him for the gifts, and pushed the furry thing towards me. I just hoped it wasn't alive.

The meeting continued with talk of agriculture, trade, and other matters. Eventually the VP stood, signaling the end of the meeting. As our guests departed and the VP made his exit, I followed him out the rear of the Roosevelt Room, headed toward his office. I noticed that the lures hadn't left his hand since he received them, but he had kindly left the furry thing for me to take care of.

An Evening with Condi

From the first minute I arrived in the White House, I realized that I wasn't like the majority of my colleagues. As I walked around the office suites located in the Old Executive Office Building, I was struck by how homogeneous my colleagues were—predominately wealthy, privileged, and white. Yes, they were all flag-waving, patriotic Americans honored to be working for President George W. Bush. Most were smart, earnest, and hardworking. Surprisingly, many were even true conservatives, rather than the "RINOs" (Republicans in Name Only) to which I had become accustomed. However, except for the large number of Latinos on staff, the number of other ethnic minorities appeared small. And black folks? Well, other than Assistant to the President and National Security Advisor Dr. Condoleezza Rice, Assistant to the President and Cabinet Secretary Albert Hawkins, and Special Assistant to the President for Economic Policy Dylan Glenn, I was the only other senior black person on staff for the president or the vice president. For that matter, I was only one of two black folks on staff working for the VP, and the only one at the time with "to the vice president" in my title.

I say this not as a condemnation of the president or the VP, but merely as a statement of fact. I had never wanted to be anything other than an eager and ambitious domestic policy aide, and the administration had certainly granted me the opportunity to do so without making me feel I had been hired for any other reason than I was smart, experienced, and loyal.

At the same time, I realized we had our work cut out for us to change perceptions in the African-American community regarding President Bush. Black folks hadn't exactly flocked to the polls to support the Republican candidate for president in 2000. In the head-to-head match-up between Vice President Gore and Governor George Bush, the vice president garnered 90 percent of the black vote to 9 percent for Bush. An article appearing in the *New York Times* summed up best what we were facing in the early days of the Bush administration:

> Another trouble spot for Mr. Bush is that there are deep and lingering resentments among black Americans toward his election. Although more than half of Americans now accept Mr. Bush as the legitimate president, three-quarters of black Americans do not. Mr. Bush's overtures to blacks in the opening days of his administration seemed to have done little to help; they say the president cares little about their needs and problems. (*New York Times*, 14 March 2001)

I wondered time and again how the Bush Compassionate Conservative Agenda could be written and implemented by a team of decision-makers who were almost entirely white. As I would discover over time, however, my toughest battles on racial politics were waged outside of the gates of the White House. What surprised me was that my first such battle would take place less than a week after I'd been on the job.

Friday, 26 January 2001. As I walked down the hall of the second floor of the Old Executive Office Building, where nearly all the vice president's staff is housed, I encountered Scooter in the hallway. It seems that in senior staff that morning, he and Condi Rice had had a discussion about yours truly. Dr. Rice had been invited to attend a reception at Howard University that evening to honor the senior black appointees in the Bush administration. As it turns out, one thing led to another in their conversation, and Condi had asked Scooter if I would be interested in attending the event with her. I was honored and flattered.

Best of all, Scooter made sure to reinforce the point that I was free to decline the invitation if I didn't feel comfortable. But he thought it might provide a chance for me to get to know Dr. Rice—an opportunity I immediately jumped at.

Later that evening, I was escorted to the first floor of the West Wing to the National Security Advisor's Office. Right on time, Dr. Rice breezed from her office with a warm smile on her face and her hand extended for me to shake. Having only seen her on television up to this point, I was struck by how elegant she looked in person.

Dressed in a gray suit with black trim, the national security advisor's attire bespoke both sophistication and class. We descended the stairs and entered her waiting car parked on West Executive Avenue. As the driver shut the doors behind us, we began our conversation. We would be attending the National Alliance of Black School Educators reception at Howard University. Dr. Rice (she insisted I call her "Condi") informed me that Secretary of Education Rod Paige would be there also. Unfortunately, Secretary of State Colin Powell had already sent his regrets for the evening; he couldn't join us.

During the twenty-minute drive through Northwest Washington to

Howard's historic campus, Condi asked me about my background and where I had grown up. We immediately clicked over a discussion about Palo Alto, my hometown, and hers too, to a certain extent.

As the provost at Stanford University (adjacent to Palo Alto), Condi knew the area and the landmarks I described quite well. Swapping stories about our educational backgrounds and what had brought us to join the Bush administration, I was immediately struck by Condi's easygoing and friendly style. Despite her power and proximity to the president, she made me feel right at home talking with her. She truly had no pretense or airs about her.

This being a blustery winter night in the nation's capital, we were both wrapped up tightly in our overcoats, so I offered to carry Condi's coat once we arrived indoors. She accepted my offer, and we passed through the doorway into the outer reception room. Little did I know that carrying her coat, combined with my being black, would set the stage for some drama inside.

Upon our arrival, many people either clapped or rushed over to meet one of the president's top advisers. Despite her stature, I wasn't sure how she would be received by the group. Given that black Republicans were few and far between to begin with, and emotions over the presidential election results were still raw with many African Americans, I had hoped that her reception would be a favorable one. As it turns out, hers was much better than mine.

As we drew closer to the podium where Dr. Rice would deliver her remarks, we were met by the official welcoming committee. Howard University's president, along with several other academic dignitaries, rushed over to say hello and have their pictures taken.

After nearly a decade of work on Capitol Hill, I knew my job was to slide discreetly to the side and allow the principal to have the spotlight.

Well, Condi would have none of that. She waved me over and was just about to introduce me to the group when the incident happened.

At this point, a well-known and senior member of Howard University approached me. This "gentlemen" told me brusquely that I could take Dr. Rice's coat and hang it in the coat check located in the front of the room. *Son of a bitch*, I thought to myself. I knew what was going on. What I had come to understand throughout my life was a simple, sad fact. In my experience, many members of the black liberal establishment could be more racist and elitist than anyone. I'm sure he assumed, seeing me (young and black) walk in with Dr. Rice, carrying her overcoat, that I was nothing more than a lackey.

Before I could even respond, Condi jumped in. No longer the engaging conversationalist, she confronted my antagonist with a tone that was far colder than the winter night outside. She pointedly told Mr. "coat check" that I was not a member of the staff, but the deputy assistant to the vice president. She admonished him to apologize to me immediately.

All this took place in front of the welcoming committee and the curious onlookers who had gathered at this point. As a nearly lifelong staffer, I was mortified: My job was not to attract attention when the principal was present. At the same time, I couldn't help but contain my glee: I am quite certain this man was not accustomed to *anyone* telling him what to do anywhere, let alone on the Howard campus where he was supposed to be the BMOC.

Responding to her stinging rebuke, the man glared at me and extended his hand to "apologize." I'm not certain of the warmth or the sincerity of his gesture, but it was an apology nonetheless. Accepting it with a smile, I imagined that the days of my receiving invites to Howard functions were over before they had even started. It was clear to me that Condi understood all too well how it made me feel. Had she thought that it was an honest mistake, I seriously doubt she would have responded the way she did.

And just like that, Condi turned back around to the group of well-wishers and posed for pictures with those who asked as if nothing had happened. Known by reputation to have a stellar intellect, she clearly demonstrated another reason the president had chosen her to be his national security advisor. In that brief moment, I had seen a glimmer of her temperament: You could sense that a general or state department official would be best advised against messing with her without being in full possession of the facts. In a world where time is a precious commodity, I had the feeling Condi would not tolerate anyone who wanted to beat around the bush or cop an attitude in her presence for the sake of being pompous.

Driving back to the White House, Condi made no mention of what I had experienced earlier. We picked up our conversation where we left off and chatted amiably all the way back. Cheerfully bidding me good night once we arrived back inside the gates, Condi was soon out of sight and back inside the West Wing. From that day forward, I was one of her biggest fans.

Conspiracy of Deputies

SHORTLY AFTER MY EXPERIENCE AT HOWARD UNIVERSITY with Condi, I attended a meeting late one evening in the Old Executive Office Building where I had my first encounter with the president's senior advisor, Karl Rove. Like most of America, I knew that Karl Rove was the mastermind behind the political fortunes and future of George W. Bush. From Bush's initial foray into politics as governor of Texas to his current position as president of the United States, Rove was behind Bush at every juncture providing strategic counsel. At this point in the early days of the administration, few of us had laid eyes upon Mr. Rove, let alone attended a closed-door session with him. This was about to change.

Room 472 of the Old Executive Office Building is often used for strategy sessions and other small meetings. That night I was present to participate in a select group that had been dubbed the "Conspiracy of Deputies." Rather than participating in an actual conspiracy or uprising, Rove had pulled together a small group of White House deputies to discuss the politics, strategies, and policies the president of the United States should be engaged in during the fledgling days of his administration. It was as if we were to be the "kids table" for Rove at Thanksgiving dinner. He presented to us the same charts, statistics, and options our "elders" were given. He wanted our unvarnished opinions.

I was more than surprised to be sitting in the room that night, as I was not a deputy of the White House or a deputy assistant to the president. Cesar had been extended an invitation in his role as the vice president's domestic policy advisor, and Cesar and I lobbied Rove's staff to allow me to have a seat at the table. I was, after all, the VP's deputy domestic policy advisor, Cesar and I argued. A stretch for sure, but sure enough, our request was granted. I was in.

I thought about what Rove would be like as we waited for him to arrive. I had heard conflicting reports on his persona, and I wanted to make a good impression during our first meeting. One school of thought held that Rove was the affable, brilliant senior advisor who was closer to the president than any other member of his staff, with the possible exception of Counselor Karen Hughes. Another warned that Rove had a quick temper and did not suffer fools lightly. Getting on his bad side could swiftly find one outside the gates of the White House without a job. I thought this characterization sounded more mythical than real, but I didn't want to take any chances with just a few weeks of White House experience under my belt.

Karl strode though the door with a smile on his face. Standing less than six feet tall, Rove has wispy blonde hair and round glasses that give him an intellectual if not owlish appearance. While I was expecting someone stern, Rove's face lit up as he made his way around the room, teasing many of the staff. When he reached me, he introduced himself and said, "Nice to meet you, buddy." Buddy? Hardly the taciturn and demanding figure I had been warned about.

As we settled into our leather chairs around the oval table in the middle of the room, Rove showed us a PowerPoint presentation with some pretty daunting statistics. Breaking the results of the 2000 presidential election out by race, President Bush had received 36 percent of the Hispanic vote and 55 percent of the white vote. As for blacks, the president had garnered only 9 percent.

Rove noted that in a two-way presidential election in 2004, should the president receive the same percentage of the vote, by race, as he did in 2000, Bush would lose the popular vote by 3 percent (3.3 million votes), lose Florida, and thus lose the Electoral College. Game, set, match.

Karl the strategist was hard at work now. Rather than focus on the next election, however, Rove challenged us to enact the policy positions and the promises that were made during the campaign. We would push the Congress to enact the president's No Child Left Behind education reform package, reduce the tax burden on American workers, reform Social Security and Medicare, and advocate long-term healthcare options while fighting to enact a Patient's Bill of Rights. In short, we would govern from the center/right of the political spectrum while trying to pass legislation on Capitol Hill in a bipartisan manner.

At the same time, the president would take his message out to the country and attract a broader constituency that would support his agenda. At this point, Karl then put up a slide that showed how the president would be a different type of conservative by outlining the so-called Compassionate Conservative agenda. There were large "balloons" and boxes depicting that we would aggressively court Latinos, blue-collar workers, Catholics, "soccer moms," and union members, I believe. At the same time, we would work to improve our outreach with the African-American community. As I was reviewing the materials in front of me, I was torn in my thoughts.

On one hand, from an altruistic and public policy standpoint, making inroads in the black community was the best thing for us to do. I felt the

Bush administration should advocate policies because they were the best things to be achieved, regardless of the votes or support they would grab. But on the other hand, there were political realities to be addressed: How much of the president's valuable time could be spent making significant inroads into the black community when the likelihood of African Americans turning out to vote for him in significant numbers was slim to none?

As the lone black man in the room, I asked myself, *Shouldn't I speak up and push for more diverse venues and opportunities for the president to pursue, since he is the president of all Americans, regardless of racial identity or politically desirable attributes? Shouldn't we expand our outreach to African Americans rather than merely seek to improve them?* At that moment, at that time, I didn't feel comfortable saying anything. I felt that if I could get to know my colleagues a little bit better, over time, I might be able to offer a different point of view regarding the president's agenda. Besides, I was presently on the staff of Vice President Cheney, not President Bush, and I didn't want to do anything that would rock the boat this early in my tenure.

Then and there, I resolved to seek every opportunity to demonstrate the value of an approach to attract the African-American community to support the Bush agenda by showing how the president's policies would benefit all Americans—particularly African Americans. What black family wasn't for education reform, lower taxes, and a streamlined retirement system with reformation of the Social Security and Medicare programs? I could find ways to demonstrate to my colleagues that we would win over tough minds and decades-old criticism of the Republican Party by playing to our strengths and boldly proclaiming how our party's policies were beneficial to all Americans rather than narrow constituencies and ethnic groups.

As Rove zipped from one slide to the next, he outlined an ambitious agenda that the president wished to concentrate on early in his term. Rove challenged us to look for ways in which we could discuss issues like education reform and cutting taxes, for example, that would project to the American people that our approach was the best one. We were further directed to look at policy and campaign pledges that were discussed and find ways to route them into the White House policy pipeline.

This last point was particularly ambitious as the president had barnstormed the country with his vision to reform education, cut taxes, and streamline healthcare while expanding the number of community healthcare centers in urban and rural areas. With the lack of a coherent energy policy in nearly twenty years, George W. Bush wanted to push an energy bill through the Congress to seek alternative sources of energy while spurring domestic production to alleviate our reliance on oil exports from overseas. The list went on and on.

This wasn't the realm of the hypothetical anymore. While George W. Bush had won a narrow and controversial election, that was behind us now. The president had to govern the country, and the president's senior advisor was asking for our help and our candid counsel to help the president do his job. Heady stuff, to be sure, but there was little time to reflect on our self-perceived importance or intellect. We had to roll up our sleeves and get to work. At this level, guesses and giving less than 100 percent wouldn't cut it. We had to be precise, we had to know our facts, and we had to know them cold. There would be little opportunity to pull back once the president announced a position or a particular course of action he wanted to take for the United States.

Leaving the meeting that night, I thought about how to proceed. First, I would focus on examining domestic issues and presenting the information to the vice president in the most objective manner possible—the job I was hired to do. At the same time, however, I would look for opportunities to share my thoughts with the vice president and members of the president's team on ways in which the Bush administration could make significant inroads in black and other ethnic communities. I would need to stress time and time again, however, that these inroads should be made because it would be the right thing to do, not because it was politically expedient. For those who were skeptical about the motives of the president and his administration as they pertained to caring about the voices and views of ethnic minorities, I wanted to do everything in my power to prove them wrong.

On the Road Again

ONE OF THE MOST UNUSUAL ASPECTS OF HOW THE PRESIDENT and vice president of the United States carry out their duties is the manner in which the two men travel to work, around town, and around the world. Unlike the citizens who elected them to office, security concerns have forced the two top leaders of the executive branch to take extraordinary precautions when they leave the White House Complex. Depending on the length of the journey, a motorcade, helicopter, or jet airplane is utilized—sometimes with a combination of all three methods in a single journey.

Sadly, the days of spontaneous presidential travel and interaction with the public are essentially over. It is hard to imagine a modern president emulating President Theodore Roosevelt, who liked to shake the hand of every constituent knocking on his door to celebrate New Year's Day, or deciding to drop in unannounced to meet with visitors at the Lincoln Memorial, as President Nixon elected to do one night during the Vietnam War. Unfortunately, there are too many people both at home and abroad who pose a security risk to our nation's top leaders. These threats have turned the executive mansion into an armed fortress and forced the Secret Service and local law enforcement personnel around the world to take extraordinary steps to protect the president, vice president, and their traveling parties when they leave the safety of the White House Complex.

During my service in the White House, I was privileged to travel around the world to deliver remarks advocating the policy initiatives undertaken by the president. Whether I traveled around the block or around the globe, I was often asked the same question time and time again by young and old folks alike: "Have you ever been in a motorcade or traveled aboard Air Force One or Air Force Two?" Without fail, when I indicated that I had been in a motorcade with both men and traveled aboard Air Force Two with the vice president, the follow-up question was always the same: "What does it feel like to be on board, and what does it look like from the inside?"

Quite honestly, the experience of travel via motorcade is unlike anything I've ever encountered. Prior to my service in the White House, I always thought a motorcade simply consisted of a series of official vehicles, with a limousine sandwiched in the middle, traveling at high velocity, American flags snapping in the wind. Over time, I would discover and appreciate with awe the numerous hours of preparation that are required to conduct a motorcade and whisk the VP or president to and from their destination. Even after all the motorcades I've traveled in, I still marvel at the precision and the ability of the D.C. Metropolitan Police, the Secret Service, and countless law enforcement agencies across the country to pull everything together.

My own curiosity about motorcades was satisfied shortly after I joined Vice President Cheney's staff. The vice president had accepted an invitation to speak before the National Association of Manufacturers (NAM) in Washington D.C. at a venue located several blocks away from the

White House. Once I heard that the VP would make the trip on the morning of 28 February 2001, I immediately sought permission to attend the event, as I was interested to see how the vice president delivered remarks before audiences and how his messages were received.

Truth be told, I also wanted to travel in a motorcade and check out everything first hand as well! After securing permission to attend, I was officially manifested on the list of those who would travel with the VP.

While there is much to tell, I'm sure the United States Secret Service will appreciate why I will not reveal too much about how motorcades are staged: Their job is hard enough as it is. Fortunately, I can report that traveling via motorcade is a fascinating and well-choreographed experience, as well as one that is performed flawlessly and coordinated with numerous offices that many people have never heard of within the White House Complex and beyond.

For example, the Office of Advance for both the president and vice president is charged with the momentous task of directing every aspect of their travel from the moment they leave the White House Complex to the moment that they return. They work closely with the Secret Service to arrange primary and alternate travel routes and ensure the vice president and traveling family members and staff know where to go (and what do) when they arrive at a particular site.

Beyond the Advance Office, both the president and vice president employ and travel with a personal aide—in my opinion one of the most difficult and unheralded jobs in the White House. For the majority of my stint on the VP's staff, Brian McCormack handled this role for Mr. Cheney. Whether placing his prepared remarks on a lectern, fielding requests from those who want "just one picture" with the vice president, or running interference, Brian adroitly handled his tasks and was often multitasking. More often than not, I would watch Brian keep the vice president on schedule—sometimes interrupting high level meetings (more typically our policy briefings) to move the boss on to his next venue.

On the night of the NAM visit, there would only be a few of us in attendance with the vice president: Cesar, Juleanna Glover Weiss (our press secretary), the VP's photographer, Dan Wilmot (head of OVP Advance), Brian McCormack, and me.

Swinging out of the iron gates of the White House, there was a motorcycle police contingent far ahead to clear traffic and block intersections for the vice president's arrival. As I discovered firsthand, police patrol cars, Secret Service vehicles, the vice president's limousine, and other support vehicles moved the vice president and his traveling party along at high rates of speed.

In typical low-key Dick Cheney fashion, our motorcade that morning did not have the sirens blazing or the support vehicles honking their horns loudly to alert other vehicles to our presence. I had heard that the VP did not like drawing this kind of attention to himself. Instead, I only witnessed the vehicles in our group flashing their lights, with the occasional honk of the horn to move people along, as we sped with minimal noise toward the Grand Hyatt Hotel.

What we lacked in noise, we more than made up for in speed and hair-raising maneuvers. I was surprised to learn that a motorcade doesn't travel in a straight line from point A to point B. Instead, the cars in the motorcade move more like a rapidly slithering snake: one minute straight ahead, the next moment veering sharply left, then right, before straightening out again. The folks behind the wheel of the vehicles in the motorcade swing left or right at a second's notice as they anticipate ways to move around other cars, pedestrians, etc., without reducing their pressure on the gas pedal.

The ride is often similar to that of a fast-moving rollercoaster, with flashing lights and an occasional siren, and I always found them to be nothing short of fascinating. As we hurried toward the event before the Business Council, I was struck by the reaction of the pedestrians on the streets of Washington D.C. For a population accustomed (if not immune) to politicians, dignitaries, and leaders of foreign governments zipping from one end of town to the other with a police escort, the reaction to the vice presidential motorcade seemed to elicit looks of awe and wonder.

After their initial shock, people usually had the same reaction time after time as we drove past: They stopped what they were doing and waved. Were they waving to Vice President Cheney? Did they think they were waving to the president of the United States? I'll never know, but, caught up in the moment, I frequently returned their waves. I'm sure we had one thing in common: The pedestrians thought the passing of a motorcade was pretty cool, and riding in the procession, I had the same sentiment—this is a *great* way to travel through the congested streets of Washington D.C.!

While we would only travel a short distance that morning from the White House Complex to the Grand Hyatt just a few blocks away, I learned that the excitement doesn't end once we've reached our destination. Security concerns dictate that neither the vice president nor his staff dawdles beyond the safety of the White House. I'm sure years ago presidents and vice presidents were able to enter leisurely through the front door, but, tragically, the likes of Lee Harvey Oswald, Sirhan Sirhan, Squeaky Fromme, and John Hinckley Jr. have dictated that the vice president and president of the United States move away from vulnerable sightlines and into cover as quickly as possible.

I can think of few motorcade experiences where, due to safety concerns, we didn't arrive below ground in a parking garage, at a back entrance way, or some other location away from the prying eyes of the public, and this particular morning was no exception. Immediately upon our arrival, all the doors to the various staff cars were flung open, and we bustled to reach the safety of the building inside. I found that staff would briskly walk with the vice president, agents from the Secret Service, and other members of the traveling party into the venue. My first day, I stayed a bit behind, primarily because I wasn't sure where to go or what to do. Dan Wilmot and his Advance team not only ensured the VP was headed where he needed to be but also rounded up errant staff like myself who were holding up the rear of the procession.

In order to minimize confusion and provide as much detail in advance of a visit, the Advance Office prepares a small booklet for the vice president and staff that provides an overview of exactly what to expect—even before departure from the White House itself. No detail is too small for Advance to overlook: time of departure, where to go upon arrival, proper attire at the event, and even the weather forecast at the venue itself were all provided for our review. I've even seen Advance place tape on the floor of speaking venues to ensure that the president and VP know where to stand at the podium.

Once inside the Grand Hyatt, we were rapidly escorted by the Advance team toward a waiting elevator that would whisk us to the Constitution Ballroom where the VP would deliver his remarks. Up to this point, I had only been in the presence of the vice president a handful of times, and I was a bit nervous to find myself face to face with him in an elevator. Despite the fact that he was about to deliver remarks to a large group, the VP looked over at me and bid me a good morning with a smile.

As the elevator doors slid open, the vice president was met by the head of the NAM, Jerry Jasinowski, who ushered him toward where Cheney would speak. The rest of the staff and I moved toward an area designated by Advance for us to view the VP in close proximity. A few moments later, Mr. Jasinowski introduced the VP to a round of sustained applause.

While I knew the National Association of Manufacturers was one traditionally aligned with the interests of the Republican Party, I was struck by the warmth and enthusiasm the group showed the vice president upon his introduction. On the heels of the president's successful Address to the Joint Session of Congress the night before, the VP was among friendly company and seemingly in fine spirits. Just moments into his remarks, the vice president introduced a joke he would use often during the early part of the year referring to himself and Speaker of the House J. Dennis Hastert as they sat just behind the president during his remarks before the Congress:

> It's one of those special evenings. You know, you're up on the podium, Speaker Hastert and I were in those chairs right behind the president, and you're on TV all the time, or you think you're going to be on television all the time, and we were a little worried that the events would be overwhelmed by our charisma. [Laughter.] But fortunately, they had a close-up of the president, and you didn't see that much, actually, of Speaker Hastert or myself. [Laughter.]

The crowd just lost it with Cheney's charisma comment. Not well known for his wit, charm, or speechmaking ability, the vice president engaged the crowd with his self-deprecating remarks.

While I had witnessed the VP's dry sense of humor in person many times before that morning, I was pleased to see he could connect with such a large audience while poking fun at himself in the process. With the audience riveted to his every word, the vice president proceeded to outline the priorities of the fledgling Bush administration, particularly the president's strong belief that a tax cut was necessary, no, overdue, to stimulate the economy. Speaking to the critics who thought the president should abandon his tax cut pledge after the historically close election, the vice president dispelled that thought by asserting:

> We had a close election, and a lot of the talking heads here in Washington said, boy, you're going to back off that tax cut—close election, obviously you're going to want to give up the cornerstone of your policy. And the president said no, I'm not going to do that. . . . That's what I think the country needs. That's what I'm going to recommend to the Congress. I'm not going to back off. And lo and behold, that's exactly what we've sent forward to the Congress.

I thought Cheney was exactly on point, and so did the audience before him, judging by their nods of assent and applause. Why in the world should the president be forced to scale back his tax cuts when that was the cornerstone of the economic policy Bush had run on? To appease the media who were so dead-set against him during the election? To appease the Democrats who had sustained such a bitter defeat? I had no doubt whatsoever that both the media and the Democrats would have scoffed if President Bush had lost the election and then cautioned the Gore White House against raising taxes. The audacity and hypocrisy of the statements on television against the president proceeding with his tax reduction agenda were appalling. I was thrilled the vice president had arrived that morning with the gloves off and facing the president's detractors squarely.

But Cheney wasn't quite finished telling those who opposed the president's tax plan where to go or how to get there.

My first State of the Union message that I watched from the floor of the House was thirty-two years ago. . . . I have never seen, in thirty-two years, as conservative a set of assumptions as we used in putting this budget together. So don't let the opposition or those who are opposed to our tax proposal, for example, suggest that somehow we're playing fast and loose with the numbers here. We aren't. We've been very conservative.

He might as well have just said, "Put that in your pipe and smoke it!"

Following a brief outline of the president's thoughts on reforming the Medicare and Social Security delivery systems, the vice president agreed to take a few questions from the crowd before we departed. Clearly in a good mood following his spirited defense of the Bush administration's initial policies, Mr. Cheney fielded questions on defense, Medicare reform, and his Inter-Agency Energy Task Force before Mr. Jasinowski drew the gathering to a close.

I had been warned to drop whatever I was doing and begin to retrace my steps out of a venue when the VP or president concluded his remarks. Indeed, veterans from this and previous administrations had told me that the motorcade or airplane waits for no one other than the president or the vice president. If you cut it close and arrive back at the car or plane after the boss is safely aboard, you can find yourself left behind and watching the rear view of the cars or the plane as they head to their next location.

Unlike President Bush, who genuinely seemed to enjoy working the rope line for extended periods of time, the vice president was more likely to wave to his listening audience and then proceed to his motorcade. This is not to say that the VP did not enjoy meeting with people—quite to the contrary. Instead, I found the VP was far more engaged in one-on-one sit-down discussions rather than pounding the flesh for long periods of time. I never confided this to anyone, but I always wondered if the vice president, for all his years in public service, wasn't anything other than shy in large gatherings. I knew the sentiment quite well myself.

Nonetheless, whether the boss worked the line or immediately headed back to the car, no staffer wanted to be left behind. That first morning, I wanted to do everything in my power to ensure I didn't. The task was all the more daunting and the timing critical as the staff had to arrive at the elevator in time to link up and ride back with the vice president. Missing the elevator would have been tantamount to missing the car, and I wanted nothing to do with that.

As we boarded the elevator, Cheney was clearly buoyed by the experience, as was I. The thrill of listening to his remarks that were so favorably received put me in a great mood, proud that I was working in the president's administration. As we rode the elevator back down to the car, the vice president looked over to me, winked his eye, and smiled. The elevator doors opened, and we strode quickly to our respective vehicles. One quick rollercoaster ride back to the White House and we were safely inside the Complex once more.

While riding in vice presidential motorcades was often a cause of excitement for me, that experience paled in comparison to a flight aboard the vice president's aircraft, Air Force Two. While I originally thought Air Force One or Two was a specific or unique plane, I would learn that any fixed-wing Air Force aircraft with the president aboard would be designated as Air Force One. The same rule applied to the vice president and Air Force Two.

On 30 April 2001, I was afforded my first opportunity to travel aboard Air Force Two as the vice president was set to deliver remarks before the annual Associated Press luncheon in Toronto, Canada. For me, this would be a special treat: Not only would this be my first opportunity to travel aboard Air Force Two, but I would also be on a flight that would take us out of the country. I wanted to soak up every last second of the experience.

At approximately 10:00 AM that day, the vice president's entourage departed the White House en route to Andrews Air Force Base. Situated just outside the nation's capital, Andrews Air Force Base is home to the 89th Presidential Airlift Group—an elite unit that is charged with the immense responsibility of maintaining and operating aircraft that carry the president and the vice president of the United States. The president flies aboard a specially configured 747-200B series plane. The military designation for the aircraft is VC-25A. The magical designation of "Air Force One" is the radio call sign that the plane uses to communicate with ground controllers and other aircraft.

The vice president travels aboard a C-32 or a specially configured version of the commercial Boeing 757. While Air Force One is limited only to use by the president of the United States, the C-32 utilized by the vice president is also pressed into service to carry the first lady and members of the president's cabinet when they travel.

Swinging around the capital beltway and into Andrews, I observed that, unlike commercial air travel, there is absolutely no delay when the vice president takes to the skies. The moment the VP emerged from his limousine, he ascended the front stairs and entered his private cabin. Those of us traveling with Cheney that day would enter the plane from the rear and make our way forward to our seats. Looking for my seat and trying not to step over the Secret Service and other members of our group, I was delighted to find a small white card with the seal of the vice president of the United States that proclaimed, "Welcome Aboard Air Force Two, Ron Christie." Pocketing the card as a souvenir, I fastened my seatbelt and took in my surroundings.

I was seated in a compartment with eight business class-type seats. I immediately dove into the fruit basket that was placed before me and smiled over at Dan Wilmot and Juleanna Glover Weiss, my friends and fellow staff members going on the trip. Dan was aware that this was my first trip aboard Air Force Two, but he played it cool as I took in the sights and sounds like a small child who was visiting the big city for the first time.

I had hardly sat down and buckled up before the engines roared to life and the plane began to move. As we straightened out on the runway and began to travel parallel to the flight line, I noticed a large number of military personnel were standing rigidly at attention. As the plane gathered speed, all the military personnel on the flight line snapped a crisp salute in unison as the VP's cabin flashed before them. With a velocity I had never encountered on a commercial flight, Air Force Two leapt toward the sky and headed north towards Canada.

Shortly following our departure from Andrews, I was surprised to see the VP emerge from his cabin and join us in ours. He spoke amiably with then Lieutenant Colonel Rich Klumpp, his military aide who was in training to assume command of Air Force Two. As he also bantered with Dan Wilmot and Juleanna, I couldn't contain myself: I grabbed my camera and took several shots. While my fellow staff members may have thought I was acting like a tourist rather than the deputy assistant to the vice president for domestic policy, the VP looked almost amused as I snapped away. Standing before me in his white shirtsleeves and red tie, Cheney asked with a smile (was that a smirk?) if I had taken a good shot. Laughing as I put my camera away, I assured him that I had—a fact that was proven incorrect when I developed my photos later. (In my excitement, I had forgotten to turn on the flash, and the pictures were a little dark.)

Nonetheless, as we streaked toward Canada, I couldn't believe I was aboard Air Force Two in the first place. Ostensibly, I was there as one of the VP's domestic policy aides who was on deck and ready to answer any questions that arose, but at that moment I felt like a starry-eyed tourist. That sensation would not last for long, as I soon discovered. Little did I know that the vice president would make headlines that day with his remarks, sending those of us traveling with him into a frenzy of activity.

Nearly two hours later, we had landed at the Lester B. Pearson International Airport-Greater Toronto Airports Authority, en route to the Fairmont Royal York Hotel where the VP would deliver his remarks. After a short drive, we pulled in under the hotel and quickly exited our vehicles. In a scene reminiscent of my first trip with the VP, I found myself rushing to make the elevator carrying the vice president and his travel party, lest I get left behind in a garage in the bowels of the hotel.

After we exited the elevator, the VP and I split company—he to participate in a photo line before the luncheon while I was escorted to table two just before the podium in the Canadian Ballroom where he would deliver his remarks. While I was exchanging small talk with my table-mates (primarily journalists from the U.S.), the VP soon entered the hall and strode to the stage where he began his talk.

With my camera once again at the ready, I had an unobstructed view of the VP as he spoke from behind a podium with a large screen projecting his image just behind him. The vice president told his audience he was proud to be part of an administration that was celebrating one hundred days in office. Cheney next launched into a spirited discussion regarding America's need to develop a comprehensive energy policy. With fuel prices rising and gasoline prices hitting two dollars per gallon in downtown Chicago, the VP succinctly outlined our deficient energy infrastructure while discussing the urgency of finding alternative sources of energy.

Up to this point, the audience of journalists appeared to either be writing in their notepads or politely taking in the remarks. As he reached the section of his remarks devoted to conservation of energy resources, the vice president made the following observation:

Now, conservation is an important part of the total effort. But to speak exclusively of conservation is to duck the tough issues. Conservation may be a sign of personal virtue, but it is not a sufficient basis all by itself for sound, comprehensive energy policy. We also have to produce more.

Around the point where the VP had said conservation may be a sign of personal virtue, I watched as the journalists around me sprang to action and scribbled furiously. Uh-oh, this could be trouble.

To be sure, I agreed with Cheney's comments 100 percent. Growing up as a youngster in Northern California, I learned to conserve water when drought conditions lowered the water tables in the reservoirs around us. Not running the water while brushing my teeth made me feel I was doing my part to save water, but it did nothing to increase the amount of water available in the reservoirs.

As previously noted, the vice president had been tasked by the president to chair the National Energy Policy Development Group, a panel that included Energy Secretary Spencer Abraham, Commerce Secretary Don Evans, and Treasury Secretary Paul O'Neill, among others, to produce policy recommendations to address America's critical energy needs. While the Group was entirely composed of government officials and therefore not open to the public during their deliberative discussions, there was a furor in the media that somehow the vice president was rewarding fat cat contributors and energy lobbyists with the report he would shortly unveil.

While I was not involved in the Energy Group's discussions, it didn't take a rocket scientist to conclude that the press and the liberal advocacy groups were looking for any type of opening to paint Cheney's efforts as nothing more than a pay-off to wealthy contributors. Was this the comment the press would spring on?

Given the murmur in the room and the frantic scribbling I witnessed at the tables around me, I decided that I had better hightail it to the staff office and tell Cesar what had happened. One of the benefits of traveling with the president or vice president is that there is often a room set aside with phones, fax machines, and other office equipment for our use. Unfortunately for me, I was having trouble placing an international call back to our office in the Old Executive Office Building. Of all the times to need a tutorial on how to place an international call!

Before I knew it, however, the Advance team told me it was time to go as the VP had concluded his remarks and had departed the stage already. Dashing out of the office and moving quickly to keep up with the group, I couldn't gauge the VP's expression. Always known for being quiet and difficult to decipher, I couldn't tell whether something was wrong or bothering him from his facial expressions. Back in the elevator and back to the motorcade we went.

Flying home, I was curious to see whether or not Cheney's conservation remarks would have an impact with the media. Like the prospectors who discovered gold in California in 1849, members of the press corps must have let out a collective cry of "Eureka!" They had just discovered the perfect avenue to attack the president, vice president, and the energy industry all at once by creating a flap over Cheney's comments on conservation. Little did I know that the vice president's simple comment on conservation would dominate the news for weeks to come.

I found the whole ruckus surrounding Cheney's remarks to be

absolutely absurd. Rather than focus on the fact that the United States relied heavily on foreign sources of oil, had an aging electricity power grid (a fact that would be proven correct during electricity burnouts in New York and California), and failed to explore domestic energy deposits such as the Arctic National Wildlife Reserve in Alaska to increase petroleum supplies, the media and the environmental lobby hitched up and girded for battle.

The missiles came fast and furious at the president and vice president in the days following Cheney's Toronto speech. The following only represents the tip of the iceberg of what we encountered. Never one to shy away from a microphone, perennial presidential candidate Ralph Nader made the following observation:

> Vice President Cheney is a dinosaur living in an age of mammals. Imagine a public official uttering the following: "Conservation may be a sign of personal virtue, but it is not a sufficient basis for a sound, comprehensive policy." It is time for the American people to insist Mr. Cheney and his fellow "oil man" President Bush that they have to wean themselves from the economically and environmentally costly energy policies that keep taxpayers, consumers, and environmentalists hooked on oil coal and nuclear power. ("A Dinosaur in the Age of Mammals, Dick Cheney and Conservation," www.impeachbush-now.org)

Where does one start with a comment like that? Did Nader somehow forget that Democrats who controlled the Congress for forty years prior to 1995 had failed to pass comprehensive energy reform? Did he also wish to criticize nuclear power as an alternative source of oil consumption when his beloved France had successfully been supplying a significant percentage of their energy needs through nuclear power?

Sadly, the arrows kept coming, and the true facts surrounding America's energy predicament lay buried beneath the reams of negative newspaper coverage. I wonder how many trees would have been saved if the press had a better grasp of the facts? That's some conservation I'd like to see.

A columnist for the *USA Today* stepped into the battleground to suggest that somehow the vice president's strategy to revitalize America's energy policy was a payoff to big business.

> So why wouldn't Cheney, who leads the administration effort to formulate a national energy plan, embrace the conservation approach? Such an idea is anathema to the National Energy Policy Development Group that the vice president commands. [Looking at the membership of the Group, the author notes that] Cheney and [Commerce Secretary] Evans are former oil industry executives; [Treasury Secretary] O'Neill once chaired Alcoa. . . . In one way or another they all have blood on their hands and owe a debt of gratitude to the energy industry. (DeWayne Wickham, opinion, *USA Today*, 14 May 2001)

Being a member of the president's cabinet and thriving in the private sector somehow makes one have "blood on their hands"? I was curious to hear what the author viewed as an honest trade, but instead he had saved the strength of his venomous attacks for the vice president himself:

> Last year, Cheney was paid a salary of $806,332 as chairman of Halliburton, a Dallas-based energy company, before he quit to become Bush's running mate. He was also given $4.33 million in deferred compensation and bonuses. Now he's returning the favor by fashioning an energy policy that will fatten the bottom line of Halliburton and many of the

nation's other energy companies. ("Conservation Doesn't Enrich Cheney's Energy Friends," DeWayne Wickham, *USA Today*, 14 May 2001)

This invective was fairly indicative of the bunk that was hurled at the administration in general and the vice president in particular. Rather than address the underlying problems such as the fact that Americans loved driving gas-guzzling SUVs that would be better suited for safari exploration on an African game preserve, many in the media tried to paint the administration's vision to address current and future energy needs as little more than a pay-off to Halliburton and energy companies. Would these detractors instead propose that we take a page from Benjamin Franklin by flying a kite with a key attached during a lightning storm to see if we could harness the power of Mother Nature to generate power in a more politically correct manner?

The Cheney conservation remarks would later serve as part of a catalyst to sue the vice president over so-called secret meetings with lobbyists and energy companies that allegedly shaped the decisions behind the National Energy Policy Development Group's work. Interestingly enough, the media coverage was surprisingly quiet when the vice president was vindicated in the courts, and calls for the VP to turn over privileged documents and communications were turned away. Who would have thought that the entire hubbub started on a day when a starry-eyed staffer took his first trip on Air Force Two to travel with his boss, the vice president of the United States, to Toronto, Canada? What a difference a day makes.

Home on the Range

AWAY FROM THE PUBLIC EYE, THE VICE PRESIDENT DISPLAYS A warm and engaging personality that would surprise even his most ardent critics. Of all my time spent on the VP's staff, I never found Mr. Cheney more relaxed and upbeat than when we traveled back to his beloved Wyoming for the Memorial Day break in 2001.

Earlier in the year, I had been tasked to look into efforts underway by the Rockefeller family to convey to the U.S. government a ranch they owned that was within the Grand Teton National Park located near Jackson, Wyoming. Upon further inspection, I discovered that family scion and founder of Standard Oil, John D. Rockefeller Jr., had purchased a 2,000-acre family retreat called the JY Ranch that the family and friends had utilized over the years.

Apparently disturbed by spreading development in the West, John D. Rockefeller had begun purchasing large tracts of land in the 1920s with the intent of turning the land over to the federal government for protection. President Franklin D. Roosevelt designated the area as the Jackson Hole National Monument, and by 1950 Rockefeller had donated some 33,000 acres that would compose the bulk of the Grand Teton National Park.

Upon his father's death, son Laurance acquired the remaining land in 1960, and as recently as 1990 had donated 2,000 acres to the park. Now in 2001, Rockefeller had decided to donate his remaining land, some 1,100 acres, to the United States to demonstrate how the public and private sectors could work together to preserve our natural resources—in this case, the Grand Teton National Park.

Vice President Cheney and Interior Secretary Gale Norton had been invited to the JY Ranch in May 2001 where ninety-one-year-old Laurance Rockefeller would sign a letter of intent to convey his land to the United States government. As the transfer ceremony would take place during the Memorial Day weekend, Cheney and his family elected to spend a few days at their home in the Jackson Hole area following the land transfer. I had been following the developments regarding transfer of the JY Ranch for the vice president, but I never expected to be asked to make the trip out to Wyoming with the boss.

While my friends on the president's staff had shared stories of utter boredom when they made the trip to Crawford, Texas, where Mr. Bush maintained his Prairie Chapel ranch, I had heard nothing but glowing reports about the beauty and wide range of activities to be enjoyed in Jackson, Wyoming. I couldn't wait.

On the evening of 25 May 2001, I found myself en route to Andrews Air Force Base where I met up with the vice president and his extended family. Taking stock of my surroundings, I observed that the vice president had been joined by Mrs. Cheney, their two grown daughters (along with their significant others), their grandchildren, and their yellow Labrador retriever named Dave.

Everyone was in fine spirits that night, and suit jackets were quickly discarded as we settled in for the flight. Dave playfully bounded up and down the aisles, and laughter from Liz Cheney's daughters rang out throughout the plane. It was as if the worries of Washington D.C. had been left behind on the tarmac once Air Force Two took to the skies heading west.

Relaxing during the flight, I started talking with Dan Wilmot and the vice president's photographer, David Bohrer, about the fun to be had in Jackson. Beautiful hiking, golf, and fishing were just a few of the pleasures to be enjoyed. With a gleam in their eyes, they had also warned me about the Million Dollar Cowboy Bar, where people sidled up to the bar and sat astride saddles rather than bar stools. Not entirely sure whether this was true or a bit of hazing on their part, I was eager to take in all the sights upon our arrival.

At one point during the flight, the vice president appeared in the cabin to hang out with the staff. Perhaps socialize is a better choice of words here. Regardless, Cheney was visibly pleased when I told him this was my first real trip to Wyoming. I told him I had stopped off in Cheyenne, Wyoming, as a little boy when we were driving across the country on a family road trip. The only thing I could remember from that trip was that my parents had bought me a pair of red cowboy boots there that I had worn so often that they were soon left in shambles. I confessed that I wanted to get another pair of boots during our trip to Wyoming.

While my traveling companions, Cheney, and the rest of the staff suppressed their laughter, they gave me the name of a boot outfit in Jackson that had a reputation for high quality boots at reasonable prices. I vowed to visit the store, Corral West, the following day and pick up a pair as a memento of my trip.

After Cheney settled into his cabin for the duration of the flight, we were treated to a hot meal courtesy of the Air Force Stewards who were graciously taking care of us. As much as I wanted to soak up all the experience of the long flight, I was soon fast asleep.

Rousing me just prior to landing, Brian McCormack, the vice president's personal aide, advised me to look out the window to witness our landing. I was surprised to hear that the Jackson Hole airport is located entirely within the Grand Teton National Park. As we descended, the majestic snowcapped peaks were prominent in the window before us and were seemingly just out of reach.

As I fixated on the peaks just outside our window, Air Force Two banked and made a swift landing on what appeared to be a rather small runway. Safely on the ground, we quickly boarded the vehicles in the motorcade and headed toward the Cheneys' property. Once they were safely inside their house, we would be free for the evening. With a wave and a smile, the VP and Mrs. Cheney disappeared into their home with their children, grandchildren, and other family members. My Jackson adventure was just about to begin.

Heading back into Jackson, we arrived at our staff hotel, otherwise known as the Snow King Resort. I was awestruck by the beauty of the hotel that was actually at the base of a winter skiing lift. My room afforded excellent views of the mountain and the surrounding forests. Since we had to rise early to prepare for the land conveyance at the JY Ranch with the VP, there was little in the way of partying that night, save downing a few beers in the Advance Office.

Early the next day, I joined Dan Wilmot, Brian McCormack, and several other staff members as we boarded the waiting vehicles to take us to pick up the vice president at his Wyoming residence some thirty minutes away. Sitting in the staff vehicle, I watched as the vice president emerged from his house decked out in a wide brim cowboy hat, dark slacks, and black boots. Minutes later, we were once again underway, en route to the JY Ranch.

Similar to the many motorcades I had experienced in Washington, this one moved swiftly and quietly, with lights flashing but sirens silent. As with our trips in the nation's capital, people appeared on the streets here and there and waved enthusiastically as we sped by. Given the prominence of Air Force Two at the airport (the aircraft was visible from miles away, silhouetted by the Grand Tetons), it was as if locals in the Jackson area had stepped from their homes to welcome their native son.

Nearly thirty minutes later, we arrived at the JY Ranch and were overcome by the sheer beauty of the Rockefeller retreat. The crisp mountain air, lush trees, and beautiful views of Phelps Lake off in the distance left many of us speechless. While the vice president and Mrs. Cheney were greeted by dignitaries including their host, Laurance Rockefeller, and Interior Secretary Norton, I peeled off with the staff to check out the stage that had been erected just days before for the ceremony that was about to take place.

A rectangular platform had been built that seemingly hovered above Phelps Lake, offering dramatic views of the Tetons in every direction. We were surrounded by lush green trees, and numerous birds could be heard chirping from innumerable perches. This was one of the most beautiful places I had ever seen.

Before long, the VP arrived at the podium where he was joined by Secretary Norton, Mr. Rockefeller, and the supervisor of the Grand Teton National Park. I couldn't help but chuckle: The dress code that day had been announced as casual, and most everyone present, including Secretary Norton, was wearing faded blue jeans. Not the boss. I suppose when you're the vice president of the United States, casual dress doesn't apply when accepting property from one of America's most prominent families on behalf of the American people.

Just steps away from the right side of Cheney, the tourist part of me overcame the professional part, and my camera was once again in hand as I began taking photographs of the event. If the VP noticed his awestruck staffer snapping photographs from just a few feet away, he didn't show it. Instead, he focused his brief remarks on the generosity of the Rockefeller family and the sheer magnitude of the beautiful oasis we were visiting that morning.

Cheney summed up what I was thinking when he noted, "This is simply the best place on earth to draw a deep breath, to clear your mind, and to appreciate the wonders of creation." With the sun just behind us and the clouds casting shadows on the crystal clear water of Phelps Lake, we were given a slight glimpse of heaven on earth that day.

As the vice president concluded his remarks and departed with Mr. Rockefeller to sit down for a private lunch, I convinced one of the Advance staff to take my picture from the short wooden podium adorned with the seal of the vice president of the Untied States where Cheney had spoken just moments before. Moments like these were too rare, I thought, to allow vanity to interfere with my desire to memorialize the scene.

Photo shoot concluded, I raced over to the cabins overlooking the lake where the vice president, the Rockefellers, and others had settled in for lunch. The Rockefellers had constructed several cabins over the years to accommodate their visiting family and friends. With an understated elegance, the cabins afforded magnificent views of the lake and the Tetons without ruining the exterior view with ostentatious material goods on the inside. This was certainly a great way to relax, if only one had that kind of money to spend.

After lunch, I reluctantly reboarded the motorcade as we bid our gracious host farewell. Little did I know that my real adventure in Jackson was just beginning.

With the Cheneys once again back in their residence early that afternoon, we were free from official duties for the remainder of our trip. While some of the VP's traveling staff retired for a nap or tried to take in a few holes of golf, I ventured downtown to fulfill the promise I had made to myself to buy a pair of black cowboy boots.

Several hours later, I returned to the Snow King armed with a pair of boots that would have made any cowboy proud—at least if he were going for the preppy, urban look. Nonetheless, I was quite pleased with the purchase, and I couldn't wait to wear them for our night on the town.

To celebrate our escape from Washington, nearly all of our traveling staff had agreed to meet for dinner and drinks at the Million Dollar Cowboy bar in central Jackson. Even Dean McGrath, the deputy chief of staff, had elected to join us for a little fun (and probably to provide a little adult supervision). Meeting up with friends from Interior Secretary Norton's Advance staff, we spent the evening shooting the breeze and some pool, as well as venting steam from the pressures placed upon us in our various positions.

As we settled in for steaks downstairs, laughter rang out in the room as Dan Wilmot, McCormack, Jose Fuentes, and others came over to admire my boots, or at least tease me for wearing them. I could not have cared less as they were extremely comfortable, and I had achieved my objective of getting the boots I really wanted.

One round of drinks turned into several others, followed by others still. As we sat and nursed our drinks, Mr. McCormack excused himself to visit the men's room. In reality, McCormack had ventured upstairs, where he either bribed or convinced a few of the local women to come back downstairs with him and play a joke on me. Sure enough, a few minutes after Brian returned, two or three women presented themselves at our table with eyes fixed only on me.

"Didn't we see you earlier at Corral West?" asked one. A more cognitive Ron would have recognized the trap that was being set, but that was not the case for me that evening. Happily announcing that yes, in fact, I had purchased a pair of boots earlier that day, one of them asked if she could see them. Discretion was clearly not the better part of valor that night.

Proudly putting *both* of my feet on the table with my black boots gleaming, I was quite pleased with myself. As they walked up to admire and touch my boots, the trap was sprung: My tablemates doubled over, clutching their stomachs with laughter. My swagger and ego sufficiently deflated, I put my feet back on the floor and accepted the ridicule that I so clearly deserved.

Still smarting as we paid our tab and headed upstairs, I soon forgot my embarrassing moments as the fun continued on. My first visit to Wyoming had really been one to remember.

Thoughts on Black America

DURING MY INTERVIEW TO JOIN HIS STAFF, THE VICE PRESIDENT told me that he paid us not only for what we knew about the issues, but also what we *thought* about them. As the weeks went by and I grew more comfortable in his presence, we soon began to have candid exchanges during our weekly domestic policy time that led me to believe he might be interested in African-American outreach. This was a topic I strongly wanted to raise with the VP, but I wanted to do so in the most effective and appropriate manner possible.

Fortunately, the opportunity for me to reach out to the vice president presented itself sooner rather than later. After our domestic policy briefing during the first week of March 2001, I found I was the last person in the VP's office after my colleagues had already filed out. As we talked, I told him that I would be very interested in sharing my thoughts on how to make positive inroads in the African-American community.

Displaying his characteristic dry sense of humor, Cheney noted that as a sixty-year-old white guy from Wyoming, he didn't have much experience in this area. This was the chance I had been looking for. I promised

to give the topic serious thought and present a memo for his consideration in short order.

On 15 March 2001, I submitted a memorandum for the vice president entitled "Thoughts on Black America." In more than two pages, I
gave what I thought was a condensed but objective outline of how he
and the president could take steps to slowly change the perception of
black folks toward the two of them. I stressed to the VP that rather than
having typical "black" events, he and the president should highlight various programs, individuals, and entrepreneurs who *happen* to be of color,
without appearing to pander to or placate the usual suspects of civil
rights leaders and clergy. I could never fully understand why Republican
strategists believed they could make progress in the black community by
sucking up to the entrenched establishment who made their living carp-
ing on the victimization of blacks in America. This was a trap I wanted
to do everything in my power to prevent the president and VP from
falling into.

Instead, I told the VP that the president could take a small but highly
important step by honoring Matthew Alexander Henson and the center that bore his name in the District of Columbia. Henson, one of our
country's greatest explorers, was the first American to reach the North
Pole with Admiral Robert Peary on 6 April 1909. I felt Henson's story
was quite compelling. As a child of former slaves growing up in rural
Maryland, he taught himself to read and eventually become an integral
part of the North Pole exploration team.

I continued by writing that the president could address an event at the
Matthew Henson Earth Conservation Corps Center in Southeast
Washington along the banks of the Anacostia River. The center was
opened in November 2000 to "promote the re-connection of Washington's
youth, particularly at-risk youth, to the wonders of nature." A center

named after a famous black explorer designed specifically to preserve the environment and staffed by young black children who were fighting to reclaim their neighborhood from years of neglect in Washington D.C.? I thought both the venue and the message would be perfect for the president's participation. Best of all, there would be no pandering, no singing and swaying "Hallelujah" event, and no self-interested civil rights leaders bemoaning the plight of black America. Just have the president, a group of proud children, and a proven program that had made considerable progress in preserving the natural environment.

Almost immediately after I had submitted my memorandum for consideration by the vice president, I received his feedback. He really liked what I had written. Speaking with him later that week, he asked me to pull together a group of black staff in the White House that I felt comfortable with so that he could hear our ideas in greater detail.

10 April 2001. Our lunch date was here. I made my way down to the first floor of the West Wing of the White House from the Oval Office to a nondescript doorway that led into a small office where three small desks were crammed together against the walls. Just outside the door, a lone Secret Service agent stood against the wall, upon which there was no nameplate or other indication of the office's occupant. Naval paintings depicting scenes and battles from conflicts long since passed hung just inside the doorway. Looking to the right from the entryway, there was a heavy wooden door with a brass handle, a door guarded by the vice president's gatekeeper, Debbie Heiden, a highly efficient woman with a friendly Texas drawl.

After I exchanged greetings with Debbie, I surveyed my lunch mates. They looked to be in varying stages of panic and nervousness. I had brought along Robert Woodson Jr. and Dylan Glenn to lend their voices to mine as we shared with the vice president our thoughts on black

113

America as well as how the administration could best reach out to the African-American community. Although they were not yet present, we would be joined at our meal by the two biggest supporters of this intimate gathering: Scooter Libby, Cheney's chief of staff, and Mary Matalin, the vice president's counselor.

Without looking up, Heiden announced that the vice president was ready to see us, and the door buzzed as I turned the brass handle to enter the room. At that point, Vice President Cheney strode from his desk to meet us. Standing on the deep navy blue carpet, we shook hands, and I introduced our guests. First up was Robert Woodson Jr., deputy chief of staff to then secretary of Housing and Urban Development, Mel Martinez. An affable man with an infectious smile, Woodson was the son of the well-regarded civic activist, Robert Woodson, founder of the National Center for Neighborhood Enterprise—an inner-city self-empowerment group. Woodson had grown up on the streets of Philadelphia and Wilmington, Delaware, to become an executive of his father's center; his was a voice of experience and wisdom about overcoming life on the streets.

Just behind Rob came Dylan Glenn. Glenn, a special assistant to the president and member of the National Economic Council, was a Georgia native, although he had attended a prestigious prep school outside of Washington D.C. for the majority of his childhood years. A former Republican nominee for Congress and barely into his thirties, Glenn was a member of the Domestic Policy Council for President George H.W. Bush. Glenn was a charmer and the consummate politician and would add an entirely unique perspective.

In the center of the room was a round, wide table with a linen tablecloth. As we took our seats around the vice president, stewards from the United States Navy entered the room and served lunch upon cream-colored Lenox china encircled by a thin gold band, with the gold seal of the president of the United States at the top. As lunch was served, Libby and Matalin joined us at the table. While my lunch mates were too nervous to touch the food on their plates, I immediately dove into my BLT and Coke.

I kicked off the meeting by telling the vice president about my childhood and background. As the son of two professional parents from Palo Alto, California, growing up in an almost all-white neighborhood, I had an entirely different childhood experience than Rob Woodson, who had been reared in urban environments in nearly exclusively black neighborhoods. As we went around the room sharing our life stories, we stressed one common theme: Just as the three of us had three entirely different backgrounds growing up, so, too, did most African Americans in the country today. We said this to point out that while Jesse Jackson, Al Sharpton, and other so-called black leaders claimed to speak with one voice, that was not only inaccurate but nearly impossible to do.

Instead, we maintained that these leaders represented the "shakedown cruise" element of black America. Finding discrimination and trouble behind every corner, these folks were extremely successful in extorting ridiculous sums of money from government and corporations that would oddly find their way into the leaders' pockets rather than the constituencies they claimed to represent.

We urged the vice president to approach outreach to the black community from an entirely different perspective than previously held by Republican administrations. Rather than the stereotypes portrayed in the media, we told Cheney, there are often more white people on welfare and public assistance than blacks. We made this statement to challenge Cheney's notion of the status quo: We enjoined him not to think of welfare reform, crime, and drugs as the issues most important to the

African-American community. Rather, we advocated that he and the president discuss the issues important to the Bush Compassionate Conservative agenda: education reform, reduction of taxes, social security reform, and the like.

Woodson, battling his nerves, but jumping into the conversation with full force and conviction, discussed at length the success the center had in numerous communities around the country by stressing self-sufficiency and finding ways to move children from failing schools so they could have the opportunity to learn and excel. Woodson stressed that blacks should strongly support the president's No Child Left Behind initiative as it promoted strict testing for children in elementary school grades. If a school failed to improve after a certain number of years, Woodson noted that many black parents would jump at the opportunity to move their children to a charter or religious school.

For his part, the vice president was very engaged and interested in what we had to say. He peppered us with a variety of questions: "What mistakes could we learn from past efforts to reach out to black people?" and "Are there particular things the president and I should and shouldn't do?" Nearly as one, we appealed to him to engage an entirely new group of people in a candid exchange of ideas. Avoiding the entrenched black establishment and listening to small business leaders, doctors, and other professionals would yield a far more accurate picture of important issues.

But we urged Cheney not to stop there: Efforts also needed to be made with community college leaders, tradesmen, and other skilled professionals. The more diverse the group, the better. By all means, no more religious swaying and prayer revivals in the East Room during Black History Month celebrations.

As the lunch neared an end, the vice president asked what should be done next. I responded that we would like to suggest places and people for Cheney and the president to visit and groups they should invite to the White House to initiate the different approach of the Bush administration to the sensitive issues facing blacks, Latinos, and other persons of color. Mary Matalin, largely silent but highly attentive during the lunch, told the vice president she agreed with everything we had said and she would help us in any way she could. Her support was extremely important, as she and Scooter Libby were the only two senior staff members in the White House at the time who worked for both the president and the vice president. Given her seniority, Matalin could introduce scheduling proposals for potential presidential participation for review and make other inroads with the president's senior staff for us.

As we made our way to the door so the VP could attend his next appointment, the vice president pulled me aside and looked me dead in the eye as he shook my hand. He said, "What I heard here today is very important to me." He continued by telling me that if I needed to see him or if there was something I thought he should see or hear, to reach out to him right away. Little did he or I know how many times I would do just that in the months ahead.

"It Looks Like a Ghetto Down Here"

My euphoria from our outreach meeting buoyed my spirits that spring. I felt as though the Bush administration would make significant inroads with constituencies that had always viewed Republicans in general, and this president in particular, with a healthy degree of cynicism. Rather than pandering, I felt as though the administration could establish a track record where our actions spoke louder than words. Just around this time, when I felt we had taken a step forward, I had a personal experience that took me two steps back.

Until 1947, the Departments of State, Navy, and War occupied what is now the Old Executive Office Building. Over the years, Room 286 served as the office of the judge advocate general of the Navy. The doorknob on the entryway door still has the naval anchor emblazoned upon it. In 2001, this suite contained the offices of Cesar Conda, assistant to the vice president for domestic policy, and me, deputy assistant to the vice president for domestic policy. Late one evening, I was putting the finishing touches on a policy memo for the vice president's review when I heard a knock at the door.

Looking up, I saw a senior member of the vice president's staff standing before me. After we exchanged pleasantries and he offered a few suggestions for my memo, which needed to get into the VP's folder prior to his departure for the Naval Observatory, this staffer dropped a bombshell that still reverberates to this day. With a smile on his face as he turned to leave my office he said, "It's starting to look like a ghetto down here." *A ghetto?* What was he talking about?

I had always prided myself that the vice president had assembled a small, intelligent, and loyal staff that rivaled the president's by way of our experience and know-how. In typical Dick Cheney fashion, he had quietly and deliberately hired who he viewed as the best group of people to put on the field; the fact that women and minorities were among the ranks of his senior staff was something I'm willing to bet the VP wasn't consciously aware of. If the best group of people available were all brown, yellow, and green by way of skin color, I have no doubt Cheney would have hired them.

Clearly, however, the skin color of the vice president's staff was something that weighed on the mind of one of our senior staff members. True, suite 286 of the Old Executive Office Building contained the office of a Filipino domestic policy advisor and his black deputy. Truer still, a few doors down the hall, Mrs. Cheney's scheduler and director of Advance, Jona Turner, was hard at work; the fact that she was an African-American woman wasn't something anyone cared about. For that matter, Jona, Cesar, and I didn't walk around consciously thinking about the color of our skin as we worked in the office of the vice president. It was all we could do to keep up with Cheney, given his insatiable appetite for information.

The ghetto? I was crushed. I wasn't sure what to think or how to react. I was angry, sad, and confused. I wanted to lash out, but I felt paralyzed to move. I had to do something.

Looking back on my outreach lunch with the vice president, I remembered that Mary Matalin had told me she was willing to help me in any way if I needed it. I needed her help now. I dropped Mary a note and told her what had happened. Her reply was nearly instantaneous and provided me with a much-needed laugh.

"He's such a goober," she said. Goober? Mary told me she would handle the situation and ensure something like this would never happen again. Handle him, she did, all right. I will not elaborate further at this juncture, but suffice it to say, the person who said this to me never deigned to make such a crass remark again during my tenure in the White House.

Run for Your Lives

LIKE MOST AMERICANS, 11 SEPTEMBER 2001 IS A DAY THAT will remain vividly etched in my mind for the rest of my life. Even now, I have difficulty explaining the events that unfolded that day as they related to me personally. How people could harbor so much hatred and so little regard for the life of their fellow human beings is a dichotomy I will never fully comprehend.

By this point, our office had established a fairly routine briefing schedule with the vice president, and we generally went in to see him on Tuesdays for policy discussions. Cesar and I had arrived early that day as our briefing time would be relatively early—approximately 9:00 AM. As I reviewed my notes for our meeting with the vice president, Cesar began shouting for me to turn on my television. At that point, the Fox News Channel was reporting that a plane had struck one of the Twin Towers of the World Trade Center. Dropping my materials and walking into Cesar's office, I watched the telecast over and over with him as we speculated that perhaps the pilot of the plane had somehow lost his bearings.

Next, the unthinkable took place. Watching in real time, the television showed a second plane heading for the other tower. As if in slow motion, we watched as the plane struck the building and exploded. We were stunned into silence. We remained silently transfixed in Cesar's office not knowing what, if anything, to say. I reasoned that if any answers were to be had, perhaps I would receive a better sense of what was going on by heading down to Scooter's office.

My friend Ethan Hastert was in an identical position as I had been moments before as I entered the office of the chief of staff to the vice president. We exchanged greetings, but Ethan's eyes remained glued to the television as we watched the replay again and again. Someone in the office told me that our briefing time with the VP had been rescheduled. With no other information available, we watched the television in silence.

Then, things really started to get out of hand, and, for the first time, I became scared for my own safety. Ethan and I had been nervously watching a plane well above the White House. We reasoned that the airspace must have been restricted, but the thought occurred to me that perhaps the planes striking the Twin Towers weren't an accident. Several minutes later, the television announced that a plane had crashed into the Pentagon. What was going on?

Returning to Cesar's office, I caught him just as he was leaving. Watching three planes strike such prominent targets as the World Trade Center and the Pentagon, Cesar had decided to return home to his family in Northern Virginia in case something happened here at the White House. With Cesar's departure, only Marie Fishpaw, our policy and research assistant, had remained in our office suite. At this stage, I reasoned that if anyone would know anything, the U.S. Secret Service would be at the head of the list.

That morning, one of my friends who served as a uniformed officer of the Secret Service and was stationed just outside of Scooter's office began waving frantically when he saw me. "Ron, you need to get out of here; I've heard there's another plane inbound to the White House and it could get here in less than two minutes. You need to get your staff, get out, and stay away from the windows." Two minutes? From where we were on the second floor of the Old Executive Office Building, it didn't take but a second to realize if a plane was heading for the White House mansion, we wouldn't even make it to the gates.

As I spun to head back down the hall, the offices containing the vice president's Secret Service detail were flung open. Men and women I'd never seen before ran out with automatic weapons. They began to shout: "Everybody evacuate the building. Get out NOW!!!" I ran back down the hall to our office to see if anyone remained. Grabbing my cell phone, I went across the hall to Legislative Affairs and sprinted back down to the corridor in front of Scooter's office where I had been just moments before.

I was scared out of my mind but still thought to call my brother. Fortunately, my call went through, and he started asking me what was going on. I told him that I didn't have any time but to call each of our parents and let them know that I was safe but evacuating the White House as a precaution. What I didn't tell him was that if the Secret Service predictions were accurate, the chances of my living to call him back were minimal. This was a sickening feeling and one that sends a chill down my spine and a twinge of nausea to my stomach just thinking about it: Was I about to die?

After working in the White House for nearly a year, I think my senses were deadened to the threat of terrorism against the president, vice president, or the White House complex itself. I felt almost lulled into a false sense of security: If the walls couldn't keep threats from the outside on the outside, surely the Secret Service could. We had heard about their extensive training, and I never gave my physical security in the building any real thought: They made me feel safe. Until now.

If the Secret Service had been anxious in trying to get us to move out of the building before, they were fully on alert and agitated at this point. The officers on West Executive Drive stood with their backs to the West Wing and yelled at us to run. Women were told to remove their heels. That phrase "run for your lives" now has new meaning to me. Running down the stairs, I looked over at Nancy Dorn, assistant to the vice president for legislative affairs, who was beside me at that point. I saw most of the VP's scheduling office in front of me, and we moved as one as we aimed for the tall black gates that had been opened for us to exit the complex.

Perhaps human nature takes over at a moment like this. Even amongst all of the chaos, I saw people reveal the true essence of their character: Some men stopped to allow women to proceed through the gates before them while others pushed and shoved to get out, blocking the escape of others.

"Move, move, move," we were told. The Secret Service was deployed on Pennsylvania Avenue with their backs to the White House, urging us to run even faster. Through Lafayette Park, we stopped to catch our breath and figure out what to do next. More Secret Service officers appeared and told us we needed to keep going north in case something happened to the White House.

In case something happened to the White House? If watching two planes strike the World Trade Center was inconceivable to me at that point, the thought of a plane destroying the White House was unthinkable. Yet, there we were, Elizabeth Kleppe, Mary Lang, Marie Fishpaw, Ethan Hastert, and I, standing at a corner, unsure of where we should go or what we should do because it was not safe to remain at the White House.

Fortunately, Ethan's brother worked in an office building nearby, and his office mates were offering their space as a sanctuary to the White

House staffers who had been displaced. Many of us were scared to enter a high-rise building this close to the White House, but we had nowhere else to go. Our cars were still on the White House grounds, and from the looks of things, we would not be returning there anytime soon.

Camping in our temporary home, I think the magnitude of what had happened sunk in for the first time. Cramped around a television, we watched as the cameras switched between the burning Twin Towers in New York and the Pentagon located just across the Potomac River from Washington D.C. There were also reports that a plane that had been hijacked had disappeared from the radar and was presumed crashed somewhere in Pennsylvania.

We were scared, unsure of what was happening, and unsure of what would happen next. Many of us were unable to raise a signal on our cell phones and could not contact our loved ones to let them know we were okay. We remained transfixed to the television and cried as we watched one tower, followed by the next, collapse in lower Manhattan. The images from the Pentagon were equally horrific, and I feared that Washington D.C. would be the next target of those who were trying to hurt the United States. With nowhere to go and little else to do, we watched television, tried to comfort one another, and tried not to think of what might happen to us.

A few hours later, Brian McCormack called one of us to announce he was safely in his apartment in downtown Washington. Brian offered his place to any of us who had nowhere else to go. Ethan and I, perhaps antsy from being cooped up for so long at his brother's office, elected to go to McCormack's apartment several blocks away.

We found the streets to be mostly deserted, save emergency vehicles and police cars that sped by. At this point in the day, I still had no cell phone signal and consequently was unable to reach my parents or brother.

Before long, we reached Brian's apartment and everyone hugged each other and then turned back to the television to hear the latest news.

I remembered a conversation with Dan Bartlett, then deputy White House communications director (and current counselor to the president), the day before in the Mess that the president would be traveling to Sarasota, Florida, for an education event at a school on Tuesday morning. Since my dad was then living in Sarasota, I remember calling him the night before to let him know the president would be coming to town on September 11.

Looking at the news, we heard that the president had left Sarasota, had landed at Barksdale Air Force Base in Louisiana, and was aloft in Air Force One once again. The networks soon aired the president's statement in which he reassured the American people that our government would track down and punish those responsible for such cowardly acts against our country.

For the first time that day, my emotions switched from sadness and fear to anger and a desire for revenge. I didn't know who was responsible for all of this, but I wanted them dead. I was brought back to reality by a call that somehow reached Ethan's cell phone. His father had been looking for him, and they were sending someone over to pick him up so he could be with his family.

As his father was the Speaker of the House of Representatives and second in line of presidential succession, they were moving Ethan to a safe and secure location. Fear once again replaced my sense of anger as Ethan and I shook hands and bid each other good luck before he was taken away.

After Ethan's departure, I felt loathe to go back upstairs to McCormack's apartment. I couldn't bear to watch the repeated images of planes striking the World Trade Center towers or the poor souls who leapt to their deaths rather than remain inside the burning buildings. More than anything else, I just wanted to go home.

Washington D.C. in the late afternoon of 11 September 2001 was an eerie ghost town, seemingly populated only by police and military officials. Civilian traffic was virtually nonexistent, and a wide security perimeter had enveloped the White House complex, making it impossible for me to retrieve my car to drive home. White House ID or not, the security cordon was not to be breached for any reason at that point. With nowhere else to go, I decided, like thousands of other Virginians that day, to point myself south and start walking home.

Never in my life have I had a deeper sense of despair and loneliness. With fighter jets screaming overhead and smoke from the Pentagon still filling the air, I felt sick to my stomach and utterly helpless. Was another attack coming? Was the first wave merely a diversion of resources so that other areas of the country would become vulnerable to attack?

Arriving home to Alexandria, I was heartened to find that my telephone was operable in my condo with the red light blinking rapidly, signaling messages from friends and family members checking on my safety. Popping open a bottle of beer and retiring to my deck, I sat down to call everyone to assure them I was all right. As the hours stretched on into the early evening, my sense of despair was once again replaced by anger. I wanted whoever did this to receive the justice they deserved, courtesy of the American military. No more coddling, no more negotiating, no more appeasing of terrorists. This was an act of war and needed to be treated as such by those in a position to do something about what had happened to America that day.

Late in the afternoon, I was relieved to hear that the president would be returning to Washington D.C. We needed our commander-in-chief making decisions from the Oval Office and not some bunker hidden away from view. The president needed to assure the country and the world that we wouldn't cower from the horrific acts that had been committed against the country. Flipping on the television, I became increasingly angry with the incessant chatter claiming that the president had looked shaky or not otherwise up to the job. Who were these people kidding?

As a staff member to the vice president of the United States, I felt shaken, upset, and otherwise out of sorts. And I wasn't even with the VP that moment, wherever it was that he had been taken for safety reasons to ensure the chain of succession of government remained intact. I wasn't even at work, and I felt a little shaky myself. But the president?

Even with the election nearly a year behind us, I couldn't help but feel the media was still out to avenge the fact that President Bush prevailed over Vice President Gore. How else could one explain the drumbeat coverage that the president somehow wasn't up to the enormous tasks that stood before us all? If anything, the president looked *human* that day, stunned when his chief of staff whispered in his ear that America was under attack, and a bit rushed when he released a brief statement from Barksdale Air Force Base in Louisiana upon his arrival. Did the media focus upon the first words uttered from his mouth? No. The president spoke the following verbatim:

I want to reassure the American people that the full resources of the federal government are working to assist local authorities to save lives and to help the victims of these attacks.

His first words were not those of anger or seeking vengeance. Instead, the president sought to reassure the American people with his first public remarks. And all the media could do was think that he looked shaky? Apparently, Bush's attempt to reassure us all wasn't good enough for them.

If the criticism of how the president looked or sounded wasn't bad enough, miraculously, members of the media began to attack the president's decision to return to Washington while also criticizing him for not returning to Washington soon enough. Consider the following exchange from Press Secretary Ari Fleischer's press briefing earlier in the day:

Q. And does the president feel hunted or in jeopardy? I mean, he is kind of trying to stay out of it?

MR. FLEISCHER: The president is looking forward to returning to Washington. He understands at a time like this, caution must be taken, and he wants to get back to Washington.

I couldn't believe my ears. Did the president feel hunted? The president was trying to stay out of it? They seemed to gloss over the fact that the president had spoken to the vice president, his National Security team, elected officials from Congress and New York State, and leaders around the world. Someone had the temerity to ask if the president was trying to stay out of things because he felt hunted? Unreal.

If the first press briefing had me angry, the second set my blood to a steady boil. Not five hours after Ari had briefed the press on the president's activities on 9/11, he stood before them once again to try to give the nation a sense of what the president had been doing. Rather than focus on the horrific acts that had been committed against the American people and our way of life, some members of the press were at it again in regards to the president's courage and decision making that day.

Q: Can you give us some idea of why the stops that we made today were made? I understand the nature of the tragedy that we're dealing with, but why these particular locations?

MR. FLEISCHER: For security purposes that involve the president.

Q: I mean, was this more like a roll of the dice as in, which Air Force bases will we end up at? Or is this more wanting?

MR. FLEISCHER: Well, of course, nobody would ever know what Air Force base we would end up at. That's routine procedure. There are a series of plans that you always hope remain on the shelf that, unfortunately, today had to be implemented.

Q: Why is he returning now?

So first he's being hunted, not wanting to engage, followed by a criticism of rapidly moving to various Air Force bases to ensure the safety of the presidency, and yet he was being knocked at the same time for actually returning to Washington. One wonders what the press wanted him to do that would elude their barbs and criticisms that day, but I felt encouraged that the president was returning to Washington and would address the nation from the Oval Office. We needed our president, and I wanted him to speak out against the evil while pledging vengeance towards those who had forever destroyed our sense of tranquility that day. War had been brought to the shores of America, and I wanted George W. Bush to fight back for all of us.

At 8:30 PM on 11 September 2001, I believe the president delivered some of his most brilliant remarks to the world under the most difficult of circumstances. In five short minutes, the president conveyed the sense of horror, sorrow, and deep resolve that showed the world why the strength and spirit of the American people would not be broken by these cowardly acts. While the entire set of remarks is too large to reprint here, I was stunned then, as I am now, by the poignant nature of the following words:

Today, our fellow citizens, our way of life, our very freedom came under attack in a series of deliberate and deadly terrorist acts. The victims were in airplanes, or in their offices; secretaries, businessmen and women, military and federal workers; moms and dads, friends and neighbors. Thousands of lives were suddenly ended by evil, despicable acts of terror.

The pictures of airplanes flying into buildings, fires burning, huge structures collapsing, have filled us with disbelief, terrible sadness, and a quiet, unyielding anger. These acts of mass murder were intended to frighten our nation into chaos and retreat. But they have failed; our country is strong.

A great people has been moved to defend a great nation. Terrorist attacks can shake the foundations of our biggest buildings, but they cannot touch the foundation of America. These acts shattered steel, but they cannot dent the steel of American resolve.

America was targeted for attack because we're the brightest beacon for freedom and opportunity in the world. And no one will keep that light from shining.

The search is underway for those who are behind these evil acts. I've directed the full resources of our intelligence and law enforcement communities to find those responsible and to bring them to justice. We will make no distinction between the terrorists who committed these acts and those who harbor them.

This is a day when all Americans from every walk of life unite in our resolve for justice and peace. America has stood down enemies before, and we will do so this time. None of us will ever forget this day. Yet, we go forward to defend freedom and all that is good and just in our world.

Immediately after the president concluded his remarks, I was surprised to find that my telephone started to ring. My surprise was increased when I found myself speaking to a senior member of the president's Domestic Policy Council staff on the other end of the line who was checking in to see if I was okay. As I began to relay the events of my day, he immediately cut me off. "The White House will be open for business tomorrow and we need you back in the office. Ron, we need you to help pick up the pieces." Up to 11 September 2001, our entire focus had been on trying to enact the president's domestic priorities such as Medicare reform and passing his tax cut package. Our entire focus would change forever that day from domestic priorities to domestic consequences brought on by the attacks on America. Still in shock over the day's events, I put the phone down and began to pick up the pieces.

As dawn broke over the nation's capital on 12 September 2001, my stomach felt as if it had been twisted into a hard knot following a night where I was hardly able to sleep. Opening my front door, I could hardly look at the front page of the *Washington Post* as I knew it contained horrific pictures of the World Trade Center from the day before. As these images were emblazoned upon my consciousness already, I couldn't bear to look at the paper or watch the news that morning.

Washington D.C. is known for having terrible rush hour traffic, but the commute in that day was extremely light. I'm sure many workers wanted things to cool down for a day or two, lest another terrorist attack take place. I was more than a little scared to be driving to work at the White House, but I was determined that my nerves wouldn't get the better of me. As it was, my parents were extremely worried about follow-up attacks, and they were convinced that the White House would be a likely target for terrorists who were unable to hit the building the day before. While I may have secretly believed in what my parents were thinking, I was determined to show up for work because I was certain there were many things that needed to get done. If for no other reason, I couldn't bear the thought of sitting in my condo with nothing but time on my hands to think and reflect about what had happened the day before.

Arriving to work that morning, I was struck and more than a little scared by the visible presence of the United States Secret Service. Ordinarily, the Service takes pains to protect the White House and its occupants with minimal visibility. Of course, 12 September 2001 was no ordinary day, and the Service was clearly making a show of force to deter any potential evildoers. Serious looking men with black outfits and long black bags were evident on the grounds and on the rooftops. I didn't want to contemplate what they were doing or what they were prepared to do. I simply entered the iron gate of the White House complex and tried to start my day.

It was hard to believe that only yesterday morning we were casually going about the nation's business in the White House. Today, we were united as a nation in mourning—scared, wounded, and not sure what this new day would bring. Would additional attacks be launched? How many people were still trapped in the rubble at the Pentagon and the World Trade Center sites? Pushing these things aside, I walked up the stairs to my office and tried to clear my head.

Once inside, I stood at the window along the rear wall and gazed out toward the West Wing of the White House. More Secret Service personnel were visible scanning the skies for threats. Old Glory had been lowered to half-staff, and a sense of sadness and despair was palpable in the air.

The first thing that struck me that morning was how nervous many of my colleagues were. Forced smiles and forced conversation dominated as we tried to pick up where we were the day before. I can't speak for anyone else, but I just couldn't concentrate on anything other than the images which kept replaying in my mind from the day before. Unable to do anything productive, I wandered into Cesar's office to take stock with him and see what it was that we were supposed to be doing.

Like me, Cesar had been sitting in his office trying to work but consumed with the nonstop television coverage. We shared what we had done after we cleared the gates and how we couldn't comprehend what had happened in New York and the Pentagon. We were particularly preoccupied by what had happened to the plane that had crash-landed in the fields of western Pennsylvania. If media reports were accurate, that plane was meant to have slammed into the White House mansion, but somehow the passengers on the plane had subdued the terrorists.

Thoughts of fleeing the day before were vivid once again in my mind. I couldn't help but wonder what would have happened if the plane had, in fact, been headed to the White House. I was certain if that were the case, I wouldn't be sitting in Cesar's office contemplating much of anything. The thought made me even sicker to my stomach than I was when I woke up that morning.

Thankfully, I was summoned to a Domestic Policy Council meeting that would snap me out of staring at the walls of my office all morning. Unlike most White House policy meetings I had attended, this one was fraught with emotion. People were hugging one another, tearing up, and otherwise venting their pent-up emotions as friends were reunited under the most difficult of circumstances.

Margaret Spellings took charge of the meeting and brought the room to order. She and her deputy, John Bridgeland, shared stories of what

Ron Christie walks with President George W. Bush during an African-American
History Month Celebration in the Red Room, 24 February 2004.

White House staff wave flags from the South Lawn as President George W. Bush and Laura Bush depart en route to Camp David, 21 September 2001.

White House photo by Paul Morse

President George W. Bush meets with Ron Christie in the Oval Office,
19 March 2004.

President George W. Bush visits with Ron Christie and his family in the Oval

Ron Christie meets with Vice President
Dick Cheney, 27 March 2002.

Ron Christie meets with Dr. Condoleezza
Rice in the West Wing, 24 March 2002.

President George W. Bush signs the Volunteers for Prosperity Executive Order
in the Oval Office, 25 September 2003.

Prior to signing H.R. 3491, the National Museum of African-American History and Culture Act, President George W. Bush meets with Ron Christie in the Oval Office, 16 December 2003.

White House photo by Paul Morse

President George W. Bush meets with Ron Christie in the Oval Office,
24 February 2004.

Ron Christie walks with President George W. Bush along the Colonnade en
route to the African-American History Month Celebration in the East Wing,
24 February 2004.

had happened to them and offered us the chance to share our stories if we wanted to. I think Margaret always regarded us as members of her extended family, and her concern for our mental well-being was touching beyond words. More than anything else, I think she knew that the people in the room and around the White House were the only folks who could relate to what we had been through the day before. Parents, brothers, sisters, and other loved ones could not fully empathize with how scared we had been when we thought we were running for our lives.

Looking around the room, I saw that many of the younger staffers were in tears. I couldn't blame them. I felt oddly cold and detached—at least they seemingly had more of a grasp on their emotions than I had. Margaret kindly advised us that there would be counselors available if anyone needed to talk about what they had been through the day before. In typical Spellings fashion, she told us not to be macho or too cool for school: If we needed someone to talk to, professional staff would be there to help us.

With those housekeeping matters out of the way, she gave us a run-down on what the president and the administration were doing to try to get things up and running again. At that point in time, this was a daunting task: The stock markets were closed, commercial aviation was all but shut down, and lower Manhattan was essentially immobilized. Margaret asked us to remain patient and try to help out in any way we could.

After we were dismissed, John Bridgeland, the president's deputy domestic policy advisor, told me to sit tight for a minute. He asked me to look into what steps would be necessary to turn Governor's Island, then a former Coast Guard base in New York Harbor, into a triage center for the dead and wounded from lower Manhattan. I promised I would look into the matter as soon as possible. Bridge (the nickname everyone called him for the more than ten years I had known him) asked me to put together a memo quickly, as he wanted the information available in order to give the president a better sense of what recovery sites were or would be available near what they were now calling Ground Zero.

Looking back now, we were all hopeful and convinced that many survivors would be pulled from the wreckage. Little did we know that nearly everyone who was unable to evacuate the Twin Towers had perished in the senseless act of murder and terrorism.

I hurried back to my desk and began researching everything there was to know about Governor's Island. Next I began thinking about how we could ferry the wounded from the City to the Island. *Ferry the wounded.* Could we commandeer the commuter ferries and press them into service as temporary hospital ships? Then, it happened again.

Cesar rushed into my office to say that we were being evacuated again. I looked into the hall and saw people running for their lives once again. Were we going to die this time? Was there another plane or other threat headed toward us? Cesar said that he was going to his car and would not be returning to the office no matter what. I took off for the gates once again and found myself spilling out of the complex more scared than I was the day before. While Ari Fleischer would later announce to the press in his briefing the following day that there had been no evacuation of the Old Executive Office Building, I knew that someone had heard something that caused many of us to run down the stairs and out the door scared to death.

Whether there was a false alarm or truly a threat heading to the White House, I'll never know. All I know is that I was terrified, uncertain of what was going on in the world, and not sure what I should do next. Should I go home? Should I go back to work? What should I do?

After my nerves were sufficiently calmed, I decided to go back to work. If there was truly a threat, I reasoned to myself, the Secret Service would do their best to protect us or at least give us ample opportunity to make a break for it.

Returning to my office, I turned my computer back on and resumed my research for the memo that Bridge had asked me for. The enormity of what I was doing hit me like a bucket of cold water. While I was scared and otherwise feeling sorry for myself, I had been asked to quickly try to assess the ability of converting space near the epicenter of the attacks in New York so that doctors and other medical professionals could tend to those who had been badly hurt. I was lucky: I was alive. The president and the vice president didn't need staff sitting around the White House feeling sorry for themselves or lamenting their lot in life. They needed all of us—the speechwriters, policy advisors, entry-level staff, all of us—to fight back the tears and get to work so they could do their jobs. If we didn't do our jobs, they couldn't do theirs. Given the totality of what had happened yesterday, to say nothing of what we would have to do to recover, I needed to get my head out of my hands and focus on the present tasks, whatever they might be.

The remainder of the week passed by in a blur. I was attending morning domestic consequence meetings that were designed to get us reoriented and moving again. I listened as topics were discussed such as whether or not to reopen Washington D.C.'s National Airport, when the ports on the Eastern Seaboard would be reopened, and how to provide technical assistance to New York City south of 14th Street. When and how would the stock market reopen for business? Could farmers use their cropdusters to spray for pests? Currently, most commercial and general aviation was grounded. Our initial domestic priorities had truly been transformed into working through domestic consequences of the September 11 terrorist attacks. Our entire focus in the White House had permanently changed, and in those first few days after the terror attacks, we sought to regain our balance and focus. For me, an event that helped ground my bearings and force me to confront my swirling emotions was the National Day of Prayer and Remembrance that took place just days after the 9/11 attacks.

Battle Hymn
of the Republic

LATE ON THURSDAY, SEPTEMBER 13, WE RECEIVED WORD THAT the president would participate in a Day of National Prayer and Remembrance. The president had signed an executive order proclaiming the same, and institutions all across America such as businesses, schools, and offices were encouraged to let folks out early should they wish to participate in a prayer or remembrance service.

On Friday, 14 September 2001, as smoke still smoldered at the site of the Twin Towers in New York and the Pentagon, a special service was about to get underway. The Cathedral Church of Saint Peter and Saint Paul, located within the National Cathedral, had opened its doors to conduct a service both to mourn the deaths of the innocents just days before and to provide comfort and strength for those of us who had lived through that fateful day.

I had mixed feelings about attending the service. Like most Americans, I was filled with sorrow for those who had been killed and wanted to inflict pain on those who had perpetrated this cowardly attack on our citizens and our way of life. On the other hand, I was scared stiff: The president and vice president would be joined that morning with nearly all the former presidents, a variety of foreign heads of state, and numerous dignitaries in the National Cathedral. If I were a terrorist, wouldn't this be the logical place to carry out a follow-up attack on America with the eyes of the entire world watching?

I have tremendous respect for the United States Secret Service and the federal, state, and local law enforcement personnel who are charged with presidential and foreign dignitary protection. At the same time, *if those folks want to hurt us and sacrifice their lives in the process, is there anything law enforcement can do to thwart an attack on the Cathedral?* I thought to myself. And then I snapped out of my self-pity party. That is *exactly* what the terrorists wanted us to do: cower, look behind our backs, and otherwise question our safety in large group settings. In my mind, September 11 was an assault on our way of life, the very freedom and sense of liberty we have here in the United States that sets us apart from so many other nations in the world. As scared as I was to attend the ceremony that morning, I did so out of a sense of civic duty and civic pride: I was proud to be an American that day, and I would not let a group of extremists intimidate me or anyone else.

With newfound courage, I boarded the charter bus that would ferry me and my fellow staffers over to the cathedral. Hardly any words pierced the heavy silence on board the nearly twenty-minute ride to the National Cathedral, located in the northwest sector of the District of Columbia. Already one of the most imposing and dominant buildings in the Washington D.C. skyline, the scene that morning was even more intimidating as we drew near. Swarms of Secret Service agents, Metropolitan Police, and other law enforcement personnel were visible on the grounds and the rooftops. Adding to the sense of heightened security, helicopters buzzed overhead and kept vigilant watch for potential threats.

Entering the building, I looked around at the hundreds of mourners who had already filled the pews of the church. As the cathedral was non-denominational, so was the group that had gathered to pray and remember the events of the past few days. Scores of congressmen, senators, and members of the Washington Diplomatic Corps were seated amongst White House staff and other members of the community.

The mood was somber and heavy as I handed my white ticket to an usher and prepared to take my seat near the rear of the large room. At that moment, Barry Jackson, a deputy assistant to the president and an old friend from my days on Capitol Hill, leaned over and handed me a red admittance ticket that would afford me a greater opportunity to observe the proceedings as these tickets were reserved for a section near the front of the chapel. Nodding my thanks, I followed the usher past the rows of mourners until I was nearly at the front of the room. Taking my seat, I took in my surroundings.

Unlike most Washington functions, this event was punctuated by sadness and silence. Glad-handing and back-slapping were replaced by silent handshakes and comforting hugs. Although I was seated with many friends who were on the president's staff, I had little if anything to say. I merely wanted to reflect on the horrific events of a few days prior while searching for the strength to get through this tragedy. I had hardly slept for the past few days, and I tried to bury myself in my work in order to bury my sense of sorrow and anger that I felt following the terrorist attacks.

Looking back now, I know that this was the first opportunity I had allowed myself to openly acknowledge how deeply the September 11 attacks had hurt me personally. I had never encountered death or experienced a near-death experience prior to this. Our culture has so inoculated us against death that when we hear about a shooting on the television or a conflict on far away lands, we can recognize that others have lost their lives, but it has little if any effect on our everyday lives.

September 11 shattered that sense of numbness for me and made me feel very vulnerable to death for the first time in my life. We hadn't been running for some fire drill or evacuation exercise; we had been running for our lives because the Secret Service was convinced a hijacked aircraft was en route to the White House in order to crash into the building and kill us. Period. The bravery of Todd Beamer and other Americans who decided to fight back against the terrorists and sacrifice themselves so others might live was something I was just now beginning to comprehend: They gave their lives so others would have the opportunity to continue living theirs. This morning, I would join the hundreds within the National Cathedral and the millions around the world who would take a moment to pray and remember those who lost their lives as a result of senseless acts of terror.

Looking around, I watched George H.W. Bush and Barbara Bush enter the room and sit in a row of pews no more than a stone's throw away from mine. There was President Clinton and Senator Clinton joined by their daughter, Chelsea. President and Mrs. Carter, Mrs. Ronald Reagan. I watched as the Prince of Wales and other foreign dignitaries came forth. Then, the two men everyone was waiting for arrived.

First, the vice president and Mrs. Cheney entered the room with their family. Shortly thereafter, President George W. Bush and Mrs. Bush strode purposefully from a side exit and made their way to their pew. Father and son exchanged greetings as the president took his seat in his pew and the ceremony got underway.

This was the first time since the September 11 attacks that I had seen the president in person. Granted, I was not a member of his staff, and my encounters with him up to that point had been minimal and incon-sequential. Yet, looking at him from just a few yards away, I sensed that he looked *different*. Sad? Yes. Angry? Undoubtedly. I couldn't place my finger on it at the time, but I'm sure that the minute he heard America was under attack at 8:46 AM on 11 September 2001, his entire life and his entire presidency changed. Knowing full well the weight of sorrow and impact the attacks had on me, I cannot imagine the weight or the burden the president must have carried to protect America from further attacks while hunting down and bringing to justice those who launched a unilateral war against us.

With everyone in place, the Processional Hymn began. For those of us whose emotions had been held in check to that point, we could not contain our sense of grief any longer. I wept, as did many of my fellow worshipers as we listened to the Processional, Welcome, and Invocation.

The first prayer was offered by Dr. Muzammil H. Siddiqi, imam from the Islamic Society of North America. Shortly after the 9/11 attacks, the president had taken to the airwaves to condemn the hatred of the attackers, but he took special pains to ensure that Americans did not attack the Islamic religion or those who followed the words of the Prophet Muhammad. Dr. Siddiqi picked up where the president had left off days before when he read the following from the Holy Koran:

> Lord, You said and Your words are true: If any do seek for glory and power, to God belong all glory and power. To Him mount up all words of purity. He exalts all righteous deeds. But those that lay the plots of evil, for them is a terrible penalty; and the plotting of such will not abide. (Holy Koran 35:10)

I was struck by the beauty and the simplicity of the words. The Lord exalts righteous acts and deeds, but He will not abide the plotting of evil acts and will punish those who do. At that moment, I was hoping the hijackers and their accomplices were experiencing some form of the punishment discussed above.

But rather than focus on anger and vengeance, the imam concluded his remarks with words of comfort, when he noted:

We turn to You, our Lord, at this time of pain and grief in our nation. We see the evil of destruction and the suffering of the many of our people before our eyes. With broken and humble hearts and with tears in our eyes, we turn to You, our Lord, to give us comfort. Help us in our distress, keep us together as people of diverse faiths, colors and races, keep our country strong for the sake of good and righteousness, and protect us all from evil.

A variety of inspirational prayers and scriptures were read to the assembled group, and we sang along with the Cathedral Boy and Girl Choristers with the text of Psalm 23 and listened to a beautiful solo performance of "America, the Beautiful" sung by Denyce Graves. The remarks of the president of the United States were drawing nearer. But first, we received a familiar but timely and poignant gospel reading from his eminence, Theodore Cardinal McCarrick, the archbishop of Washington. McCarrick chose a reading from Matthew 5:2-12a to set the stage for the sermon from the Reverend Dr. Billy Graham and the remarks from the president:

Then He began to speak, and taught them, saying: "Blessed are the poor in spirit, for theirs is the kingdom of heaven. Blessed are those who mourn, for they will be comforted. Blessed are the meek, for they will inherit the earth. Blessed are those who hunger and thirst for righteousness, for they will be filled. Blessed are the merciful, for they will receive mercy. Blessed are the pure in heart, for they will see God. Blessed are the peacemakers, for they will be called children of God. Blessed are those who are persecuted for righteousness' sake, for theirs is the kingdom of heaven. Blessed are you when people revile you and persecute you and utter all kinds of evil against you falsely on My account. Rejoice and be glad, for your reward is great in heaven."

I wanted to applaud the cardinal's remarks, but I knew doing so would be entirely inappropriate in this setting. Yet, he touched upon nearly every sentiment I felt but had been unable to express or articulate with any clarity. I felt deep anger towards those who falsely claimed they had attacked the United States in the name of God. I took solace in the words that called for the blessing of those of us who mourned while finding a blessing in the knowledge that those who had been persecuted due to some perverse sense of righteousness on behalf of the terrorists had, in my mind, found solace and sanctuary in Heaven.

As Cardinal McCarrick concluded his remarks before the hushed audience before him, an enfeebled and weak man took his place at the rostrum. While clearly in ill health, the Reverend Dr. Billy Graham spoke to us in a strong voice about the evil that had befallen the country while imploring us for the strength to move ahead.

Next, a visibly distressed George W. Bush took to the rostrum and spoke from his heart while delivering some of the most eloquent and poignant remarks uttered during his presidency. He opened by praising the acts of decency and kindness displayed by rescue workers and passengers on an aircraft who faced and found death by trying to save the lives of others. But beyond the warm words for those Americans who had sacrificed their lives to protect others, Bush also had a message for the terrorists who had senselessly murdered thousands of Americans:

Just three days removed from these events, Americans do not yet have the distance of history. But our responsibility to history is already clear to answer these attacks to rid the world of evil.

War has been waged against us by stealth and deceit and murder. This nation is peaceful, but fierce when stirred to anger. This conflict was begun on the timing and terms of others. It will end in a way, and at an hour, of our choosing.

Fidgeting in my seat, I found myself nodding in agreement with the president's thoughts. While I didn't have the luxury of time or history to put the 9/11 attacks into context, I knew that those responsible would hear from America in a way they could never have imagined. While they might have landed the first punch through trickery, I hoped the president was right that we would end the battle at a time and place of our choosing.

But rather than limit his remarks to expressions of anger and vengeance, the president touchingly reminded Americans that while we had much to be thankful for, we should still seek God's love, protection, and comfort in difficult times, as he noted:

America is a nation full of good fortune, with so much to be grateful for. But we are not spared from suffering. In every generation, the world has produced enemies of human freedom. They have attacked America, because we are freedom's home and defender. And the commitment of our fathers is now the calling of our time.

On this national day of prayer and remembrance, we ask almighty God to watch over our nation, and grant us patience and resolve in all that is to come. We pray that He will comfort and console those who now walk in sorrow. We thank Him for each life we now must mourn, and the promise of a life to come.

And we have been assured, neither death nor life, nor angels nor principalities nor powers, nor things present nor things to come, nor height nor depth, can separate us from God's love. May He bless the souls of the departed. May He comfort our own. And may He always guide our country.

With tears in my eyes, I looked up as the president left the stage and returned to his seat. Touchingly, I could see that the president's father had leaned over to squeeze the hand of his son with pride and adoration. We were not presidents and ambassadors, heads of state or VIPs that morning. Instead, we stood shoulder to shoulder in a place of worship seeking comfort for the actions of a few evil men who sought to change the course of our country and our ways of life forever. We were united in our resolve not to let the cowardly actions of a few cower us or deter us from our pursuit of peace, justice, and freedom.

At the same time, we concluded the ceremony, appropriately I thought, by singing the "Battle Hymn of the Republic." Make no mistake: While ours was a forgiving God and this was a ceremony designed to heal and recover from the terrible acts of evil, we left that day with a message for those who sought to harm us once more:

Mine eyes have seen the glory of the coming of the Lord;
He is trampling out the vintage where the grapes of wrath are stored;
He has loosed the fateful lightning of His terrible swift sword;
His truth is marching on.

I have read a fiery gospel writ in burnish'd rows of steel;
"As ye deal with My contemners, so with you My grace shall deal";

Let the hero, born of woman, crush the serpent with His heel;
Since God is marching on.

He has sounded forth the trumpet that shall never call retreat;
He is sifting out the hearts of men before His judgment-seat;
Oh, be swift, my soul, to answer Him! Be jubilant, my feet!
Our God is marching on.

Glory! Glory Hallelujah!

As our voices rang out in unison, I felt deeply moved inside. This was exactly the form of therapy I needed, even though I would never have admitted to myself at the time that I was in pain and in mourning. With a skillful mix of prayer, reflection, and song, we were challenged to pick up the shattered pieces of our lives and move forward with resolve.

Life in the Cave

Inspired by the moving ceremony at the National Cathedral, I was trying to adapt to the rapidly changing world both inside and outside of the White House. From a professional standpoint, changes were underway following the 9/11 attacks that made our jobs on the vice president's staff anything but routine.

For one thing, for security reasons, the president and vice president of the United States would rarely ever be in the same place at the same time for months on end. Prior to the attacks, the vice president and the president worked extremely closely together. The vice president had attended many of the same briefings and meetings as the president prior to September 11. Sadly, this was no longer the case: In the aftermath of these attacks, extraordinary security measures were put in place to ensure the whereabouts of the two men were only known by those who truly needed to know.

Prior to September 11, for scheduling purposes, I had access to the vice president's daily calendar and his projected activities over a two-week period of time. Following the attacks, only limited senior staff in the vice president's office were privy to such information, and I was no longer one of them. Moreover, access to the West Wing of the White House itself was now strictly limited. Only those deemed essential to business in the West Wing were issued new navy and gold passes with a yellow outline around them. While I retained my ability to come and go from the West Wing after 9/11 as a member of the vice president's staff, I felt constrained to enter the building only when attending a meeting, briefing the vice president, or picking up a takeout order from the White House Mess.

It wasn't that I didn't want to go to the West Wing. Instead, I felt as though the atmosphere of the entire place had changed from being an open and inviting work space to a serious War Council. And for good reason: The United States had been attacked without warning or provocation, and those charged with providing the president with information and alternative courses of action did not have time to deal with idle chitchat.

For example, before 9/11 the Staff Table in the White House Mess used to be a place for mid- and senior-level staff members to sit down over a meal, blow off stress, and share a good laugh. Senior staff such as Chief of Staff Andy Card or Senior Advisor Karl Rove used to plunk down with the rest of us to get acquainted and otherwise catch up on the latest news. Immediately after 9/11, the staff table remained deserted, along with most of the remainder of the dining room, with staff either unable or unwilling to be seen in the Mess taking a break.

The ground level of the West Wing had turned into a whirlwind of activity. At nearly any moment of the day or night, dark Chevy Suburbans might appear to deposit the secretary of defense, secretary of state, or attorney general at the White House for a meeting with the president or other key officials. I'm convinced Card and others wanted to keep as many people out of the way as possible as the United States struggled to regain its footing, and I didn't want to be perceived as being in the way if I could avoid it. Besides, in the Old Executive Building we had more than enough things to keep us busy as we kept the vice president abreast of the latest developments.

As mentioned above, in order to preserve the continuity of government should the White House be targeted for attack, the months following the September 11 attacks would rarely find the president and the vice president in the same place at the same time. While this may have preserved the succession of government from collapsing on paper, this imposed separation between the president and the vice president had a somewhat chilling effect on our staff. Oftentimes, only the most senior staff who worked for Mr. Cheney knew where he was and how long he would be there. The media began to note that the vice president was often in a "secure and undisclosed location," a place that I joked to Cesar should be dubbed "the Cave." Days would pass where the president was in the White House while the VP was off in the Cave.

Some of us on the VP's staff questioned not whether we would be attacked again, but when. This led to questions about the safety of working in the White House. Do the terrorists have a dirty bomb or something similar that they could hurl over the gates of the White House? If they did, could we get out in time?

These thoughts were rarely out of my consciousness in the first several weeks after the 9/11 attacks. To compound my fears, I soon discovered that there was nothing more unsettling to hear than that the national threat level had been raised, and that as a precaution the vice president had been taken to a "secure and undisclosed location" away from the White House. To me, this meant that the danger was such that in case the White House was attacked, they wanted the vice president far enough away from Dodge that when the dust settled, he would still be alive. As for the rest of us . . . ?

The more difficult days were the ones in which I heard that the vice president had been moved either before or while I was driving into work that morning. Even worse were the days that we were already at work when Cesar or another member of the staff would excitedly burst into my office to announce: "The Boss [VP] just left the West Wing and hopped into a motorcade headed to the Cave." Lovely. Nothing better to raise my spirits than to hear that it was deemed too unsafe for the vice president of the United States to remain in his office, and yet I was deemed nonessential enough that I was to remain at my post.

While I don't think any of us would have consciously admitted it at the time, those of us who did not travel with the vice president when he departed to the Cave were extremely jealous of those who were thought important enough to make the journey with him should Armageddon strike the White House. From an emotional and psychological perspective, this was a very difficult reality for me to accept. Trouble brewing? Vice president and essential staff depart, Christie remains.

After a time, my self-pity subsided, and I realized that the vice president needed every last one of us to focus on the job at hand. We had a tremendous amount of work and information that we needed to sift through, and Cheney needed us to do our jobs rather than worrying about perceived slights or insults.

While the September 11 attacks may have altered the way the White House conducted its business, the vice president tried to tend to his in much the same manner as before, to the best extent he could, given the circumstances. For the domestic policy staff, this meant Cheney's insatiable appetite for information needed to be addressed: He expected the usual deluge of memoranda and other information to be completed and submitted for his review. From a logistical standpoint, the paper flow was easy enough for us to manage. What proved more difficult was the ability to sit down with the vice president on a weekly basis and brief him in person as we had done thus far. With the VP in the Cave more often than not after 9/11, we were given a solution: We would conduct our weekly briefings via video conference.

Looking back on the experience, I found briefing the vice president in the weeks and months following the 9/11 attacks to be one of my most difficult duties during my three-and-a-half-year stint at the White House. At the designated time, we would file in and situate ourselves around a table and wait for the vice president to appear. I had a running battle in my mind whether the scene from our policy briefings looked more like an interview with Ted Koppel on *Nightline* or something one would expect to see on *Star Trek*. Shortly after we were seated, the vice president's face would magically appear and fill an entire projection screen that dominated the room.

While most of us had grown comfortable briefing Cheney on our activities in person during peace time, this was an intimidating proposition. A staccato round of questions could arise that you didn't have the answer to, or you could find yourself less prepared than you wished. Finding yourself seated in a video conference room with the face of the vice president being beamed in while he was trying to help the president put things back together, with the White House and the country in a virtual state of war, took intimidation to new levels. With the vice president's time now being one of his most precious commodities, he had little patience for the staffer who was unprepared to fully engage during our limited domestic policy briefings.

While we were all under an almost suffocating amount of tension and stress as the fall turned to winter in 2001, there were still ample opportunities for us to let off steam and make light of our unique working conditions. Rather than drink or engage in other self-destructive behaviors,

I took every opportunity I could to mask my fears and vent pressure via jokes and humor. One incident in particular stands out in my mind that involved Mr. Cheney himself that occurred sometime late in the year.

We were surprised one day to find that we would actually be conducting our domestic policy briefing in person with the VP in his West Wing office. Over the course of that briefing, the vice president (as he was wont to do) was razzing me about something or another. For some reason, I had always had a big target sign painted on my face that Cheney seemed to zero in on and tease me when the mood struck him. I learned to ride the thin line between being respectful and sarcastic, and I soon learned to dish back to Cheney when he would tease me.

In any event, the VP took a moment that morning to razz me about something during our briefing, and I decided to zap him right back by asking him if he had seen the skits *Saturday Night Live* had recently been running about him on their show. When he said that he hadn't seen the skits, I saw an opening to tease him by promising to return with a recent recording of a *SNL* skit that parodied Cheney's life in the Cave.

Often known for their caricatures of presidents over the years, comedian Darrell Hammond had perfected his imitation of the vice president and his mannerisms to near perfection on *Saturday Night Live*. In one particular episode that I had fortuitously recorded, the comic had portrayed a bare-chested Cheney located in a "secure and undisclosed location" with his heart doubling as a coffee brewer. At one point in the skit, the mock Cheney reaches over for a mug and pours himself a cup of coffee from his heart/dispenser. I roared with laughter along with the studio audience as the character on the screen remained calm, cool, and collected while tooling around in a cave bare-chested.

I thought I could share the tape with the vice president without being insubordinate or crossing a line, and, fortunately for me, the VP shared in the fun and told me after watching the tape that he had found it very funny as well. For several weeks, I found myself recording *Saturday Night Live* and bringing the tapes into work if the VP was parodied.

My attempts to razz the VP in these stressful times did not stop at *Saturday Night Live*, however. One day I was reading the *Washington Post*, and editorial cartoonist Tom Toles had a scene in which Osama bin Laden, hiding from the Coalition forces that had been searching for him, decided to dig a deep cave to elude capture. In the cartoon, the bin Laden figure notes: "If I just dig my cave a little bit deeper . . . Uh-oh, Vice President Cheney!" At that point, the wall of dirt falls, and bin Laden is nearly face to face with the vice president, buried and hidden in the middle of the earth in his safe and undisclosed location.

I found the barb too good to pass up, and I clipped the cartoon out and saved it for one of the rare opportunities when we would brief Cheney in person. Sure enough, one day the opportunity presented itself, and I brought along my cartoon hidden in my briefing folder. As we wrapped up our session, I reached for the cartoon and handed it over wordlessly. Scanning the cartoon, Cheney's face broke out in a smile and he shook his head while returning the cartoon to me. While these may have been the most trying of times for all of us, being able to keep a stiff upper lip while also being able to laugh proved to be an invaluable tool to get us through the worst of our fears and uncertainties as we pulled things together to move on with our lives.

A Call to Service

As the American people rallied around their president and their country, a new spirit of patriotism was noticeable everywhere. A nation bitterly divided after a contentious presidential election had pulled together to show solidarity and unity following the 9/11 attacks. Partisan rancor in the Congress was low and enlistments in the U.S. military high as people from all walks of life, ethnic groups, and socio-economic demographics were drawn together to prove to the terrorists that their acts of cowardice did little to diminish our love for our country or our resolve to pull through these most difficult of times.

In the months following the 9/11 attacks, the White House received countless letters and phone calls and other outpouring of support offering to help in any way possible. As a member of the vice president's staff, I was asked by friends, neighbors, and even strangers how they could help the country.

President Bush sought to sustain the new culture of service, citizenship, and responsibility that the American people so willingly displayed. Unbeknownst but to a handful of aides, the president decided to issue a national Call to Service during his State of the Union Address in which he would call on all Americans to commit at least two years (or four thousand hours) over the course of their lives in service to others. He further created a new White House office called the USA Freedom Corps to facilitate meaningful volunteer opportunities for Americans seeking to answer his Call to Service. As he made this new call to service, the president noted in his remarks that:

> None of us would ever wish the evil that was done on September the 11th. Yet after America was attacked, it was as if our entire country looked into a mirror and saw our better selves. We began to think less of the goods we can accumulate, and more about the good we can do.
>
> For too long, our culture has said, "If it feels good, do it." Now America is embracing a new ethic and a new creed: "Let's roll. . . ." We have glimpsed what a new culture of responsibility could look like. We want to be a nation that serves goals larger than self. We've been offered a unique opportunity, and we must not let this moment pass.
>
> This time of adversity offers a unique moment of opportunity—a moment we must seize to change our culture. Through the gathering momentum of millions of acts of service and decency and kindness, I know we can overcome evil with greater good. And we have a great opportunity during this time of war to lead the world toward the values that will bring lasting peace.

Listening to the president's remarks on television, I was struck by this new call to service. I thought it remarkable that a Republican president had called on the Congress to expand the AmeriCorps program (long derided by conservatives as a liberal boondoggle), double the number of Peace Corps volunteers serving around the world, and supplement the nation's first responders with a volunteer initiative called Citizen Corps.

I thought the initiative was a great idea and one that would allow for meaningful opportunities for those Americans young and old who sought to serve. I was curious to see how many people would respond to the president's Call to Service and whether he could harness the strength and energy of the American people who sought avenues and outlets to serve their country.

Little did I know that in just a few short weeks, I would be called upon to channel my strengths and energies to serve in the president's community service initiative and, much to my sadness, leave the vice president's office.

During the day of January 29, the day of the State of the Union, John Bridgeland, the president's deputy domestic policy advisor, had pulled me aside to tell me that there would be a big announcement during the speech. Bridgeland further asked that I listen carefully to the remarks and promise to touch base with him the following day. Promising to do so, but not sure what I was looking for, I heard about the USA Freedom Corps that night along with millions of other Americans.

The following day, Bridgeland called me over to his office on the second floor of the West Wing to tell me that the president had asked him to take the helm of this new office and serve as the first director of the USA Freedom Corps. As I congratulated him on this exciting news, Bridgeland was not quite finished with me. He asked me to join him and a small team he was putting together to run the USA Freedom Corps.

I was flattered by the offer, but I had no desire to leave the vice president's staff. Over the course of nearly a year, I had overcome my doubts and insecurities and felt I was just hitting my stride as Cheney's deputy domestic policy advisor. The months following the 9/11 attacks had drawn the already tight group of the vice president's personal staff even closer together. While I had always dreamt about joining the president's staff someday, I didn't feel this was the time personally or professionally to make the move.

Then Bridgeland told me he was set to travel with the president later that day to Florida to promote the USA Freedom Corps, and he wanted me to consider his offer to join his team. While he couldn't make any promises without conferring with the president, Bridge felt confident that I would receive commission as a special assistant to the president of the United States—a position I had dreamed about for many years while working on Capitol Hill. Suddenly, I was eager to rush back to my office and tell Cesar about my conversation with Bridge, but I was sworn to secrecy, lest the vice president or Scooter scuttle any potential move.

Leaving Bridgeland's office, I was truly stumped as to what I should do. On one hand, I had always wanted to serve the president of the United States as a member of his staff. The vice president's office had been an amazing experience up to this point, but I wanted to see if I had what it took to advance the president's agenda more directly as a member of his team. On the other hand, I was distraught about the prospect of leaving the vice president's office. Cheney, Scooter, and the rest of the team had shown me nothing but respect and appreciation for the work that I had done thus far. Most of all, I felt a personal loyalty and bond with the VP himself that I did not want to relinquish. I felt that the vice president had taken a personal interest in my professional development, and I had learned an immense amount from him. This was not going to be an easy choice to make.

The next day, I found myself back in Bridgeland's office. This time he started to put the screws into me and press for an immediate decision: Would I make the jump or would I stay with the vice president? I stalled for more time and told him I needed the weekend to think things over. After reluctantly giving me the time I requested, I left Bridge's office and, leaving the Old Executive Office Building, ran into Margaret Spellings, who greeted me with a simple, "Take the job, Ron." Great, no pressure. Just the president's top domestic policy advisor and someone for whom I had a great deal of respect telling me to get off the dime and take a new position.

Crossing the street later that afternoon to grab a snack at the Mess in the West Wing, I happened upon Karl Rove as I entered the building. With a large smile on his face, Rove walked up to me, put his hand on my shoulder, and said, "Dude, take the job and come join us." Returning Rove's smile with one of my own, I told him that I was flattered and was seriously thinking about joining the team, but I hadn't made up my mind just yet. Thankfully, he didn't press me further on the matter and went on his way.

Reviewing my situation, I think Bridgeland was wise to the fact that I felt I could turn down his offer without feeling too guilty about it. Spellings and Rove, however, presented an entirely different story, and I believe Bridge had pulled out all the stops for me to join him in this new venture for the president.

Returning to the VP's office, I couldn't keep my situation secret any longer. I walked into Cesar's office, told him I needed his advice, and shut his heavy wooden door behind me. After catching him up on all of the activities related to a potential position in the USA Freedom Corps, Cesar was adamant that I couldn't leave.

"C'mon, man," he started. "Think of how cool we have things in the VP's office. The boss likes you, and we have free reign to do what we need to do to help him. You get to go on the plane, take trips, and travel with the boss all the time. Things will be different if you join the president's staff. You might not ever get to see him." Cesar's remarks perfectly targeted the angst I was feeling.

I *did* have a pretty amazing work portfolio and supportive environment in which to do my job. I had regular access to the VP, we got along well, and I enjoyed the esprit de corps that we had working for Mr. Cheney. Moreover, I was worried that despite Bridge's promises of Oval Office briefings and direct access to the president, I could just as easily find myself never seeing the man or having any meaningful interactions with him. This was very important to me as I had always been in positions on Capitol Hill, including Senator Allen's campaign for office and my current position with the vice president, in which I was able to interact and learn from the principal himself. The many special assistants to the president that I knew had told me in the past that they almost never saw the president or were in a position to brief him.

Playing devil's advocate to Cesar's position, I responded that the USA Freedom Corps would present me with a golden opportunity to help build something important. The president was trying to tap into the enormous swell of patriotism to do something special for those who were willing to serve their country. While I wasn't a big fan of the AmeriCorps program at the time, I thought the president's vision to double the number of Peace Corps volunteers serving around the world was admirable. While I wasn't entirely sure what the Citizen Corps initiative was all about, the prospect of increasing the number of communities served by Neighborhood Watch, creating a Medical Reserve Corps to supplement first responders around the country, and creating an Operation TIPS initiative within the Justice Department where concerned citizens could alert authorities about suspicious activities seemed like an amazing office to be a part of.

"I want to be in on the ground floor of this," I told Cesar. "Maybe they'll let me stay on the VP's staff and join the president's team just like Mary and Scooter are doing." This seemed to mollify Cesar a bit. Mary

Matalin and Scooter Libby were the only two staff members in the White House to serve on the staff of both the president and the vice president. Since a precedent had already been established with those two, perhaps they might make an exception for me as well, I reasoned.

Promising to take this option up with Bridge on Monday morning, Cesar and I parted ways for the weekend. Over the course of the next two days, I consulted my family and closest friends as to what I should do. Their verdict was a unanimous one: Take the job with the president! I knew in my heart of hearts that this was the best decision for me professionally, but my personal affection for the vice president and his team was strongly tugging at me not to leave his office. Ultimately, I reasoned with myself that I would never again be presented with an opportunity to create something in the White House and help lead an important initiative for the president of the United States while our country was at war. Staying with the vice president was the safe choice, but joining the president's team would allow me to try to make a difference more directly. I planned to announce my decision when I returned to the White House on Monday.

After a mostly sleepless night on Sunday, I rose earlier than usual and went into work to get the deed over with. One look from Cesar as he poked his head into my door confirmed that I was wearing both my emotions and my decision on my sleeve: "Damn, you're leaving, aren't you?" he asked. With a nod, I told him that I was going to take the new job but try to stay on the VP's staff as well. My phone began to ring shortly thereafter, and John Bridgeland was on the other line. I told him I had reached a decision, and I wanted to tell him in person what I had decided to do.

Entering his office, I told him I wanted to join his team, but I had a few questions to ask first. Was I really going to be commissioned as a special assistant to the president? If so, could I remain on the VP's staff as well as join the president's? To this second point, Bridge was emphatic in his answer: "No, Ron. You can't do both. I need you to help me get this off the ground, and I can't have you split between the two staffs. If you're going to do it, you're going to have to leave Cheney."

Damn. To make matters worse, Bridge needed my answer immediately as White House Chief of Staff Andy Card was set to swear in the next class of commissioned officers the following day. In order for me to join that group in the Roosevelt Room for the ceremony, Card would have to take the matter up with the president and meet with me beforehand. The sands in the hourglass were up for me: I had to make my decision.

With a heavy heart at the prospect of leaving the VP but elated to help launch the president's new community service initiative, I reached over to shake Bridge's hand and tell him I was in. With that out of the way, I had two more people I needed to speak to: Scooter Libby, my chief of staff, and the vice president himself.

I left Bridge's office to find my friend Jenny Mayfield, Scooter's executive assistant and right hand. I told her that I needed to speak with Scooter right away, but the nature of my conversation was confidential and I didn't want to reveal what I had to say in advance. Jenny told me she would do what she could and get back to me.

Late in the day, Jenny called to announce that Scooter was free to see me. Ushering me into his office, Scooter asked me what was up that I needed to see him so urgently. While he always had had an open door policy with the staff, one-on-one meetings with Scooter were extremely rare as he was always busy and on the run. Wearing the hat as the vice president's chief of staff as well as his national security advisor didn't leave Scooter with much time for idle chitchat in the office. Out of deference for his schedule, the VP's domestic policy advisors had always gone to Dean McGrath, the deputy chief of staff, for policy guidance and other help.

Forcing myself to relax, I relayed to Scooter everything that had tran-spired over the past several days regarding the USA Freedom Corps opportunity. In his customary fashion, he didn't interrupt me while I spoke, but his gaze remained intently fixed upon me. When I finished and told him that I was excited by the prospect of taking the new job, Scooter finally began to speak.

He told me that he was sorry that I wanted to leave the VP's staff, but he said that the new job sounded rather exciting. Without directly trying to dissuade me from my decision, Scooter asked if I had had any problems with staff in the office or if there was another reason why I had wanted to leave. Assuring him that this was not the case, I told him I wanted to help build something for the president and the country with this new opportunity.

Graciously, Scooter asked if I would consider staying on the vice pres-ident's staff as well as joining the president's. He wasn't sure if Andy Card would allow me to do so, but Scooter said that he and the vice pres-ident were happy with my work and he didn't want to lose me. Scooter had always been nice to me during my time in the vice president's office, but I had never been told I was doing a good job or otherwise received an "atta-boy" from him. That was his style. If one did something wrong, that was another matter. But Scooter expected us to do our jobs and not sit around looking for praise. The fact that Scooter had so openly told me that he was pleased with my work and had offered to keep me on staff while at Freedom Corps touched me deeply.

Unfortunately, I told Scooter that Bridge had told me already that splitting my responsibilities between the two staffs was not an option. If I wanted to go with the Freedom Corps, I would have to leave OVP. Shaking my hand and congratulating me on my decision, Scooter asked when I would join the president's staff. I responded that Card was set to swear in the next group of commissioned officers tomorrow evening. "*Tomorrow?*" he asked. "Tomorrow," I replied. "In that case," Scooter continued, "you'll need to tell the vice president, but he isn't here at the moment. I think you might have to try him on the plane."

This news shattered the sense of calm that I had felt up to this point. While Cesar and Scooter had been gracious about my decision, the prospect of telling the vice president I was leaving his staff on the phone was one I did not relish. In fact, the thought of calling him on the plane scared me to death. Would he be ticked off or would he be pleased for me?

Never having contacted the vice president while onboard Air Force Two, I wasn't sure what to do. Scooter told me to call the signal operator and ask to speak to the operator on AF II. Sure, I thought, that will never work. Back in my office, I did exactly as Scooter had instructed me.

Within seconds, a voice identifying itself as the Air Force Two operator accepted my call. "Hi, this is Ron Christie calling. May I speak to the vice president, please?" To my surprise, a few seconds later, Cheney cheerfully picked up the line. Had Scooter told him anything?

For the third time that day, I shared my decision and how I had arrived at it. Not surprisingly, he was gracious, and he congratulated me on my decision. He then asked when I was going to be sworn in, and I told him the following day. He replied that he would be returning to Washington D.C. shortly, but I should go ahead and accept the position. He said he and I could talk about this in person upon his return. Thanking him for the honor of being a member of the team, I replaced the phone in the cradle and pumped my fist in the air. Thank God the boss approved of my decision!

The following day, Tuesday, 6 February 2002, I arrived in Secretary Card's outer lobby with Stephen Garrison. Garrison, a former policy staffer for Governor Bush, had been serving as the special assistant to

John Bridgeland. Later that evening, he and I would be sworn in as special assistants to the president, but Card had asked to speak with us beforehand. While Card had always been friendly in my encounters with him in the Mess or around the White House complex, I didn't know him all that well, and I had little idea what to expect from him in our meeting. Was this meeting merely a precursor or technical formality to our being sworn in as members of the president's staff, or was there a possibility we still had to interview for our positions? Not knowing the answer to either question, I was comforted by the fact that Garrison and I would be going through this process together.

Stephen Garrison was one of the friendliest staffers in the White House, and he and I had bonded quickly during domestic policy council meetings. A graduate of Stanford University, Garrison had returned home to Texas to work with Governor Bush before joining Bush's 2000 presidential campaign as a policy aide. Now a member of the domestic policy council staff and just in his twenties, Garrison was about to be one of the youngest commissioned officers to the president. As we sat and bantered back and forth in Card's outer office waiting for him to usher us in, my nervousness slipped away.

Before long, Melissa Bennett, then Card's executive assistant (and current deputy assistant to the president), told us that the chief of staff was ready for us. Entering the room, one is struck at how impressive the chief of staff's office looks. Several large windows are adorned with gold drapes that hang from the ceiling to the floor. Off to the right side, several bookshelves are interrupted by a working fireplace in the center of the wall. To the left are several couches and chairs for smaller meetings and a full conference table for larger gatherings. Just inside the door to the left is the chief's desk, behind which is a door leading to a private terrace. You could almost *feel* the power emanating from the room.

Card warmly greeted us both and motioned for us to take a seat. Dispensing with pleasantries, the president's chief of staff began a nearly thirty-minute conversation in which he touched on the historical and special significance of being a commissioned officer. Unlike any other staff in the White House, commissioned officers were appointed directly by and worked immediately for the president of the United States. Similar to the discussion I had heard in my early days on the VP's staff, Card reinforced that we served at the pleasure of the president of the United States—for the time being. We were cautioned that the president's pleasure could end at any point and that the time of our departure might not be along the timeline we imagined. "Don't get comfortable," Card warned us. "I expect most people will serve in these positions for no longer than eighteen months. This is not a place to have a career. You give 100 percent to the president and the country and then you move along to do something else outside of the government." Just when I thought our new jobs couldn't sound any more bleak, Card suddenly switched both his tone and his demeanor with us.

He reminded us of both the honor and privilege it was to be appointed by the president to undertake such a position. He stressed that most people who sought to be commissioned officers would never attain such a position. With that in mind, we were reminded that we would be a direct reflection on the president by how we acted and treated others. We could not be too respectful or courteous to our colleagues in the White House and the people we would meet outside the gates as we carried out our duties.

Finally, Card stressed how we would receive access to the president. "If you need to see the president of the United States, I will make sure that you see him," he told us. "If you merely *want* to see the president of the United States, you will not see him." We weren't hired to hang around the president and bask in his aura. Instead, we were about to be appointed by the president to serve the American people and not get caught up in the trappings of our office or get too big for our britches.

And there would be pressures on us that could change even the most humble among us, we were told. All commissioned officers to the president are formally addressed as "Honorable." Before long, I was told, I would see invitations addressed to "The Honorable Ron Christie." Courtesies would also be bestowed upon us similar to those accorded to general officers in the armed forces. We would be senior enough to rank the use of an official car and driver as we carried out our responsibilities during the day. And for many, the best perk was membership to the White House Mess, the small and exclusive dining room staffed by the top cooks and stewards in the United States Navy.

After expressing our excitement and honor at being selected by the president to serve, Garrison and I stood up to leave. Card thanked us for our commitment and promised to see us later that evening for the ceremony. For me, the evening couldn't come soon enough.

Ordinarily, the Roosevelt Room serves as the president's conference room and the location of senior staff meetings each morning. That evening, the long round table had been removed, and many of the chairs placed to the rear of the room, which had been filled with selected guests and fellow commissioned officers. In all, twenty-four of us were about to take the oath and begin our new assignments on the president's staff.

The breadth and diversity of my colleagues was impressive, if not a little intimidating. To my right, retired Army General Wayne Downing waited with the rest of us for the ceremony to unfold. Legendary for his service as the head of the Army Special Forces, Downing was to be sworn in as a deputy national security advisor on Dr. Rice's staff. Over there stood H. James Towey, who had served as general counsel to Mother

Teresa and had run the Health and Services Agency for the State of Florida. He would assume the top job in the president's Faith-Based and Community Services Office. Distinguished lawyers, corporate leaders, and former military officers were just a few of the careers my colleagues had had before now. In all, I was thrilled to join this group and a touch on the insecure side: Do I measure up to these guys?

At about this point, Secretary Card entered the room and asked us to be seated. In a reprise of the conversation he had with Garrison and me earlier in the day, Card reminded us of the honor and privilege to serve the country. Almost as if he had read my mind, Card told us that it was not a mistake that we had arrived here: Each of us had unique qualities and strengths that would be counted upon by the president to carry out the agenda of the American people. He urged us to work hard but not to get too wrapped up in our jobs. We were implored to make time for our spouses, significant others, family members, friends, and neighbors. Keeping our grounding and bearings would help us advise the president to the best of our abilities.

After his inspirational remarks, we were asked to rise and lift our right hands. As we swore an oath to protect and preserve the Constitution of the United States, I was nearly overcome by emotion. I had always dreamed about serving the president of the United States, and now I was being given my chance to work hard and try to make a difference. I would not let them down for choosing me, I vowed!

As we finished taking the oath of office, Card walked around the room and shook the hands of the twenty-four newest members of the president's team. Before he let us go, Card assembled us before the fireplace in the Roosevelt Room beneath the portrait of President Theodore Roosevelt astride a rearing horse. Tina Hager, one of the White House photographers, had arrived to take a photo of our group, which remains one of my favorite keepsakes to this day. With Card standing in the middle of a beaming group, Hager captured one of the happiest moments of my life. A few weeks later, the picture arrived in my office with the following words inscribed at the bottom: "To Ron Christie—It is our honor to serve with you on the President's team. Sincerely, Andy Card."

While I was newly sworn in as a special assistant to the president, I had promised Scooter and Cesar that I would juggle my new position with my current one until a replacement could be found for me. Having given those two men the courtesy of my intentions, I still had to sit down with the vice president to discuss my decision. As gracious and supportive as he had been to me, I felt that I had an obligation to outline my decision to him in person.

Just a few days after I had been sworn in on the president's staff, I received word that Cheney was free to meet with me. I was more than a little nervous as I crossed West Executive Drive and ascended the stairs to the second floor of the West Wing. Before entering Cheney's office, I met a confrontational Debbie Heiden, the vice president's executive assistant. "What's this I hear about you leaving, Ron Christie?" As I started to explain, she smiled and told me that she was proud of me and that I had better not become a stranger. With that, the VP's door buzzed, and I was free to enter.

With a smile on his face, the vice president of the United States walked over to shake my hand and ask me to take a seat. He told me that he respected my decision to take the new spot, but that he would miss me on his team. As if he were reading my mind about my obvious discomfiture, Cheney gently added that it was an honor to him that the president and his team thought highly enough of me that they wanted me to join the president's staff. Finally, Cheney told me before I left that

I had done good work for him and that I was always welcome to return to work for him if I ever wanted to.

I was deeply moved and nearly overcome by the desire to hug this man who had taken a risk in giving me the opportunity to serve and work on his staff. Should I thank him for being more of a mentor than a boss? A swirl of thoughts went through my head before I told him that I was honored to have been a member of his team and I wouldn't let him down while working for the president. Shaking my hand again before I left, Cheney patted me on the shoulder and led me to the door.

Over the next month or so, I remained split between the office of the vice president and the USA Freedom Corps. Slowly but surely, however, my duties were weaned away from me on Cheney's staff as the weeks went by. My participation in our weekly briefings gradually decreased as the baton was being passed, and I gradually transitioned out.

Finally, the day I had dreaded arrived in early March. With my files neatly placed on the bookshelf in my office, I turned in all my equipment and door key. Sighing and looking out of my window for the last time, I watched the American flag flutter on the flagpole atop the White House building. I wanted to leave this office the same way I had entered it: alone. Finally, I shut my door, walked out, and headed down the checkerboard tiled floor of the Old Executive Office Building. My new responsibilities awaited me in Jackson Place, the site of my new office, and it was time to get to work on the president's community service initiative full-time.

Packing up my possessions from the office of the vice president, I left the comfort and security of the White House gates to set up shop with my colleagues in USA Freedom Corps at 736 Jackson Place, which is one of the townhouses lining Lafayette Park. One underreported fact of life for White House staff after the 9/11 attacks was that offices on the western side of the Old Executive Office Building had to be closed; that side of the building was susceptible to a truck bomb or other high explosive devices. As a result, offices such as Presidential Personnel, the Faith-Based and Community Services Offices, and others would have to be located in temporary quarters, like the townhouses of Jackson Place, while the Old Executive Building was being reinforced and restructured.

For those of us in USA Freedom Corps, we were only a stone's throw away geographically from the White House. However, it seemed like a posting to Siberia for those accustomed to rubbing elbows with the movers and shakers in the West Wing. Nonetheless, 736 Jackson Place was our beautiful and historical new home. It had also been the temporary home of the twenty-sixth president of the United States. Nearly one hundred years to the date prior to our arrival (June 1902), President Theodore Roosevelt and his family had moved across the street to 736 Jackson Place while the White House renovations that resulted in the creation of the West Wing were underway. Later in the year, Roosevelt would help negotiate a deal between striking coalminers and their union leadership from Pennsylvania from a front office on the second floor of the building that would become my office.

We also had our own work cut out for us in these historic times. Launching USA Freedom Corps and the president's community service initiative along with it required us to have staff sent over (or detailed) from several federal agencies with programs or projects that related to the work we were doing. The president had charged his fellow citizens to devote at least two years or four thousand hours of service over the course of their lifetime serving others. He had called for the creation of a Citizen Corps to help mobilize thousands of volunteers as well as the establishment of the Medical Reserve Corps, Volunteers in Police Service program, and an expanded Neighborhood Watch program to help supplement and support our first responder and law enforcement communities. Here we were fortunate to call upon detailees from the Federal Emergency Management Agency (FEMA), the Department of Justice, the Department of Health and Human Services, and the Corporation for National and Community Service (CNCS) to join our team and offer their specific subject matter expertise.

With the president's call to double the number of Peace Corps volunteers serving around the world in five years, we called upon that agency's director, Gaddi Vasquez, to make his staff and their expertise available to us. Finally, with the president's commitment to raise the number of AmeriCorps participants serving in the nation's communities from fifty thousand to seventy-five thousand, as well as increasing by a hundred thousand the number of Senior Corps members, our new detailee from CNCS (the parent agency of these programs) helped us navigate landmines and fulfill the president's service commitments.

Beyond Stephen Garrison and me, who were serving as special assistants to the president for USA Freedom Corps, Bridge had also hired Lindsey Kozberg to serve as our communications director—the identical position in which she had been serving at the Department of Education. All in all, our numbers were small and our responsibilities enormous.

While the president's domestic and international community service goals won him wide praise from Republicans and Democrats alike on Capitol Hill, I knew that we had major challenges in the days ahead. For one, the AmeriCorps program was not popular with many conservative members of Congress and their staffs. Just a few years earlier, I had been a strong advocate of the elimination of the AmeriCorps program as I thought the results achieved were low while the cost of running the program was extremely high.

While proponents lauded AmeriCorps members as "volunteers," I chafed at this label as their education stipend and other benefits paid for by the taxpayers reached well over ten thousand dollars for each member. Throw in child care and other services, and the program's costs could climb even further. How in the world would we convince two chambers of Congress controlled by conservative Republicans that expanding the AmeriCorps program was the right thing to do?

Of course, my personal opinions at this point were not of any real importance: I was charged by the president of the United States to expand the AmeriCorps program, and I would attack my assignment with zeal. Unfortunately, I would learn over time that the president's Call to Service was resisted both inside and outside of the gates of the White House by conservatives who were skeptical of Bush's service initiative.

In the first few weeks following the president's announcement, reaction within the White House itself remained rather positive. Our communications director was invited to the internal White House message team meetings, and Stephen Garrison and I were welcomed to attend the Domestic Policy Council staff briefings as equal participants.

For his part, John Bridgeland had been promoted from being a deputy assistant to the president to being an assistant to the president—elevating Bridgeland to the president's senior staff, which met every morning at 7:30 to discuss the president's schedule and events that were likely to shape the news that day. Most important, as an assistant, Bridgeland was permitted to submit scheduling proposals and advocate that the president travel the country and discuss his Call to Service.

At the same time, there were those inside the gates of the White House who snickered at my decision to leave the vice president's staff to help lead the president's service initiative. "Are you crazy?" I was asked time and time again by members of the president's team. "Why in the *world* would you, of all people, be out there promoting the AmeriCorps program?" Most difficult of all, I found myself asking the same question over and over again.

Created by President Clinton in 1993, AmeriCorps places thousands of young Americans in rural and urban communities around the country where they teach school, help build homes, and otherwise engage in civic activities. Shortly after the program's creation, it was attacked by conservative Republicans on Capitol Hill who believed that the program was bloated and mismanaged and that its participants engaged in partisan political activity against Republicans. I welcomed efforts on Capitol Hill to terminate the AmeriCorps program in the mid- to late-1990s. Now I was one of the president's senior advisors on how to *expand* AmeriCorps from fifty thousand to seventy-five thousand participants? My conservative friends in the White House weren't quite sure what to do with me.

Even more perplexed were my former colleagues who were still serving as legislative aides on Capitol Hill. It didn't take long for my friends to find out that I had left Dick Cheney's staff—a man still lionized in the House of Representatives as being a staunch conservative—to join the president's team to defend a program most conservatives detested and found unfathomable.

As I had contemplated whether or not to join the president's team, I found myself doing some deep soul-searching. While I deplored the AmeriCorps program in its current form, I strongly believed that the president could lead the way in implementing reforms that would run the program more like a business than a feel-good operation. If we could insist on strict accountability as to how money going into the program was spent, reduce administrative costs, and eliminate partisan political activity on the part of AmeriCorps participants, perhaps we could help bring the program into favor with conservatives after all.

I was willing to take the chance of having my conservative credentials questioned, if not tarnished, because I genuinely believed that the president shared similar goals for reforming AmeriCorps while at the same time providing an outlet for the thousands of young Americans who were looking to serve their country in the days following 9/11. I felt that I owed it to the president and myself to see if we could turn things around. Besides, my boss at USA Freedom Corps was suspected on Capitol Hill of more likely than not being a liberal. If I could help smooth things over on the Hill with our conservative friends, so much the better.

Our first few weeks at the USA Freedom Corps Office were spent trying to add substance and structure to the president's articulated Call to Service. How does one expand AmeriCorps from fifty thousand to seventy-five thousand participants in one year in the face of heavy Republican opposition on Capitol Hill? In practical terms, was there enough interest both at home and abroad to double the size of the Peace Corps over five years? And all these Citizen Corps programs—wasn't Bush just looking to increase the size and scope of government when the Republican-controlled Congress was trying to *decrease* the size of government? This was not going to be easy.

While Lindsey Kozberg focused on our communications message and Stephen Garrison set out to launch the various components of Citizen Corps with our staff detailed over from other federal agencies, my job took me in two distinct but related directions.

First, I sought to build support within the White House and on Capitol Hill for obtaining the president's service commitments. Adding tens of millions to AmeriCorps and the Peace Corps was met with resistance on either end of Pennsylvania Avenue. Conservatives could hardly understand why the president would want to aggressively promote and fund a service agenda. My job here was to educate where necessary and, in conjunction with the White House Office of Legislative Affairs, cut the deals necessary to bring legislation to the president's desk that would fulfill his funding and legislative objectives.

At the same time, Bridgeland decided to deploy me as an ambassador of goodwill for the USA Freedom Corps. No city was too large or small for me to fly to at a moment's notice to deliver remarks in support of the president's Call to Service. I would also discover over time that these same ambassadorial duties would reach back into the White House itself as the AmeriCorps program soon found itself faced with financial, political, and management problems that would sour even the most loyal of Bush staffers in the building who viewed AmeriCorps as nothing more than an albatross that was dragging the president down.

My conservative credentials were presented early and often to skeptical members of Congress on Capitol Hill who dreaded the president's community service initiatives. During the week of 4 March 2002, I felt like a piñata at a children's birthday party as I was batted around both chambers of Congress by elected officials whose views of the president's service agenda could be described as hostile, or lukewarm at best.

First up for me was the majority leader of the House of Representatives, Richard K. Armey (R-TX). Armey, a retired economics professor, was well regarded in conservative circles for his attempts to reduce the size and scope of government. A strong ally of my old boss (former Ohio Representative and Budget Committee Chairman John Kasich), Armey had supported efforts to eliminate the AmeriCorps program altogether. Now I was being sent into the lion's den to try to convince Armey to support the president's expansion plans, rather than oppose them.

Unfortunately for me, Armey had been tipped off about my having worked for John Kasich in the past, and his opening words hit home as I walked into his spacious Capitol office. "Weren't you one of the guys who was trying to shut down AmeriCorps when you were up here?" Armey greeted me. "Yes, Mr. Leader," I responded. "But you haven't heard about the president's vision to reform the AmeriCorps program."

I was instantly on dangerous ground at this point. On the one hand, I had been in deep discussions with Bridge and other staff in the White House about ways that we could reform the AmeriCorps program. On the other hand, we were still in the discussion phase and had not sat down with the president to brief him and receive his authorization to move forward. Golden rule number one in the White House was that we were *never* to be out in front of a position or policy unless it was a position or policy endorsed by the president of the United States. Freelancing was one of the quicker ways White House staffers could find themselves on the outside of the gates looking into the building and yearning for their old jobs.

While I was not advocating a position that ran counter to the president's, I needed to reel things back, lest the majority leader presume I was articulating policy that had already been signed off in the White House. Instead, I told Armey that we all believed AmeriCorps was expensive, and we needed to ensure the taxpayers' dollars were being spent as wisely as possible. I continued by noting that the president was developing principles to reform the program that would be unveiled shortly that would make the fiscal conservative members in the House very happy.

At this point, John Bridgeland, who had accompanied me, and David Hobbs (Armey's former top aide who was now serving as the deputy assistant to the president for legislative affairs) interjected to ask if the president could count on Armey's support for the president's community service expansion plans. I had known Bridge for nearly a decade at this juncture, and he has always been a bright, hard-working, and earnest man. However, there are times when being hard-working and earnest can run counter to the best ways to enlist the support of a powerful member of Congress best known for being crusty and an avid crusader against liberal causes and big government spending. Bridge's direct appeal for support made me cringe. I braced myself for the outburst that was surely to come.

Instead, Armey took his time to measure up and gaze at his guests before replying to Bridge. Armey told us that he wouldn't support expanding the AmeriCorps program as that would upset many members in the House. At the same time, if we rounded up enough members to vote for an AmeriCorps bill (218 votes are required for a majority vote in the House of Representatives), Armey told us he would not block the bill from reaching the floor. This was a huge victory for us; we had been given assurances that the president's planned expansion of AmeriCorps would proceed through the House if we rounded up sufficient votes.

When we heard this, David Hobbs and I nearly leapt to our feet as one to head for the door. The outcome was far better than we could have predicted, and it was best to quit while we were ahead. We thanked the leader for his time and were about ready to go when I noticed that Bridge was still seated and talking to Armey. Not good.

Having the majority leader willing to let a bill move to the floor was almost as good as him agreeing to support it. Given that the majority leader chooses which bills will reach the House floor for a vote and which will be sent to the graveyard where they die without receiving any consideration, we had achieved our objective. Any rationalizing or trying to convince Armey to actively support the president's plan could lead us down the wrong path. Unfortunately, I couldn't come right out and say that to Bridgeland, my boss, who outranked me by two levels in the White House hierarchy. Instead, by placing my hand firmly on his arm and thanking Armey again for his time, my boss got the message we were leaving.

As we were in the corridor outside, Hobbs told us he would follow-up with his old boss to ensure we would be given a vote if we rounded up enough members to support us (218, to be exact). Heading back to the car, Bridge asked me why Hobbs and I were so quick to leave. Much to his surprise, I told Bridge that it was difficult to gauge the level of distrust if not outright hatred of the AmeriCorps program in conservative circles. Having been there myself just a few years earlier, I told Bridge that all the rationalizing in the world would not change the mind of many conservatives when they heard the word "AmeriCorps." Anything after that word gets drowned out as the members starts thinking about liberal crusaders sitting around a campfire singing "Kumbaya." I should know, as I often had the same reaction myself.

Instead, I told Bridge that we would only win this fight by appealing to conservatives under the notion that we would reform the program, insist on results, and measure the progress of what program participants were supposed to do versus what they were actually able to accomplish. Otherwise, I concluded, our boat would be sunk.

For his part, Bridge appeared to be very appreciative of my counsel. I promised to keep my finger on the pulse of the conservatives if Bridge vowed to support me if I told him we needed to talk to or make certain concessions to the conservatives to make the notion of voting for AmeriCorps more appealing. With this agreement in place, we went back to the White House to prepare for our meeting with Senator McCain the following day—a meeting that would prove far more taxing than our encounter with Dick Armey.

At 1:30 PM, Bridge and I found ourselves in Room 241 of the Russell Senate Office Building, suite of the senior senator from Arizona. Tastefully decorated, there was no question about the fact that McCain represented a state full of southwestern charm. What was more of a question, however, was how McCain would react to our visit. While press accounts had proclaimed President Bush and Senator McCain remained friends following the 2000 presidential election, I had my doubts.

McCain had been gathering momentum in early 2000, and he was stopped by a Bush victory in the South Carolina primary only after a vicious campaign that proved to be the beginning of the end of McCain's candidacy. Less than a year ago, McCain supporters had claimed that Bush and his team had made slurs about McCain's fitness to serve. Now, here we were, sitting in McCain's outer office to seek his support in helping Bush draft legislation that would advance a key priority of the president's. They say that politics makes strange bedfellows, and we were about to find out if McCain would be supportive in our endeavors.

A few minutes later, we were ushered into McCain's personal office for our meeting. I had met the senator once or twice before in my career, and I had always found him to be warm and engaging. Today was no exception, as he graciously welcomed us and invited us to sit down. With his tanned complexion and well-appointed suit, McCain looked very much like the senior senator, confident and in control of the situation.

The senator listened to us for several minutes as we sketched out some of the reform plans that we had for the AmeriCorps program. As McCain was a senior member of the Senate Health, Education, Labor, and Pension (HELP) Committee that had jurisdiction over the AmeriCorps program, we had come to him to sound out his willingness to serve as the lead sponsor of the president's reform package. To my surprise, McCain wasn't entirely happy once we had finished our presentation. Oh, he supported the president's goal to expand the AmeriCorps program from fifty thousand to seventy-five thousand participants, all right. Problem was, he felt that we weren't going far enough: He thought the number and the scope of the program should rise even further!

In the clipped and measured tone that is well known to millions of Americans, Senator McCain told us (or was he lecturing us?) about the unique period of time the country was in. McCain was a strong supporter of the president's Call to Service, he told us, but he wanted the president to set greater targets for young people to participate in programs such as

AmeriCorps and the Peace Corps. Listening to Senator McCain's take on the president's Call to Service, I was stunned as to what to say or think.

While there might be enough support to pass a bill with higher target/funding levels for the AmeriCorps program in the Senate, there was no way such a bill would see the light of day in the far more conservative House of Representatives. I had my doubts about whether Senate Republicans could even stomach an AmeriCorps bill at all. Given that many of the solid-right conservatives in the Senate had served in the House of Representatives when the fever to eliminate the AmeriCorps program had burned in the mid-nineties, I wasn't so sure we would pass anything in the Senate—particularly not at higher levels than called for by the president.

But what was I to do? Senator McCain, seasoned legislator and beloved war hero, was on a tear about how the president should proceed. I didn't think it was my place to remind him that a larger AmeriCorps bill wouldn't fly in the Senate and surely wouldn't pass in the House of Representatives. Perhaps Bridge, who was seated next to me, would chime in to remind Senator McCain of the political winds that were blowing in strong opposition to the president's plan to expand AmeriCorps. No such luck.

Bridge and I listened to a very pleasant McCain outline *his* vision and *his* thoughts on what a service agenda should look like. I truly felt like we were between a rock and a hard place now. House Republicans still wanted to gut the AmeriCorps program, President Bush wanted to expand it, and Senator McCain thought Bush hadn't gone high enough! This was going to be an interesting spring as we tried to herd members of the House and Senate of all differing political stripes to agree on a bill that would reach the president's desk.

Filing out of his office after McCain vowed to support us in any way he could, I knew we were in for some rough sledding. I told Bridge as much, and he cheerfully told me we would get this done and make conservatives happy by reforming the program and liberals pleased with strong Republican engagement on community service. While that might be true on paper, I thought we wouldn't have much of a prayer of accomplishing our goals without the president's strong, direct, and personal involvement in our efforts. Would Bridge be willing to fight that fight with his colleagues in senior staff who were so protective of the president's time and focus?

A few weeks later, I started to have my doubts. On 20 March 2002, I found myself nervously awaiting my first formal briefing with the president of the United States. Bridgeland had asked for time on the president's schedule in order to brief him on our meetings on Capitol Hill as well as to receive his approval to release a document detailing the president's vision for the AmeriCorps program. While Bridge would lead the briefing for our team, I was to be "on-deck" should the president or senior staff have any questions that I could help answer.

While I was comfortable briefing and even bantering back and forth with Vice President Cheney, I was petrified by the prospect of being grilled by the president of the United States. True, I had always dreamed of briefing the president and having him rely on my advice on some pressing matter of the day, but the reality of being in the Oval Office itself and looking at the most powerful man on earth while speaking coherently was a terrifying proposition. What if he didn't like what I was saying? What if I was nervous and didn't make sense? These thoughts were running through my head, and I wasn't even slated to formally brief Bush that day.

When the moment of truth arrived, we walked to the White House for our 4:00 PM briefing. Bridge told me to feel free to jump in at any point if he had missed something, but he was going to give the president an update on how the Freedom Corps initiatives were coming along and report on our meetings with members of Congress and the vision document we wanted to circulate on the Hill articulating the president's vision of reform for AmeriCorps.

As we made our way closer to the Oval, I was convinced everyone could hear how loudly my heart was beating. From out of nowhere, a sheen of perspiration appeared on my forehead. The temperature on the first floor of the West Wing is always cool, but my body started to overheat due to my fear or excitement of the impending briefing. Telling myself to relax and focus, I took a deep breath as we rounded the corner and stood just outside of the president's suite of offices.

Located in the southeast corner of the West Wing and overlooking the Rose Garden, the Oval Office is the formal workplace of the president of the United States. Rather than making myself even more nervous by focusing on the historical significance of the room itself, I tried to keep calm by focusing on the task at hand: Follow the conversation, and be prepared to jump in if necessary. These thoughts were swept aside as we were told the president was ready for us.

Entering the Oval Office for the first time, I was overwhelmed by everything before me. The president of the United States was seated almost immediately to our right in a blue-and-gold-striped armchair set before the fireplace in the rear of the office. Flanking Mr. Bush on the right and left were two cream-colored couches on which some of the most recognizable faces in America were seated. Karl Rove, Andy Card, and others were arrayed on the couch and chairs to the president's right. We walked around the back of the couch to the president's left, walked across the presidential seal embedded in the rug atop the wooden floor, and settled in just to the president's left side. On the coffee table in front of us was a beautiful array of freshly cut flowers, which gave the room a pleasant aroma.

I had always assumed meetings in the Oval were intimate affairs with just a few aides present. That day I was shocked to discover that there were nearly a dozen people in the room. As we walked inside, the official White House photographer began clicking away and capturing the moment on film. Here goes nothing, I thought.

While this was not the first time I had met the president while at the White House, this was my first meeting with him as a member of his team. As I settled in, George W. Bush welcomed me with a warm smile and a wave. This greeting had the effect of settling my nerves a great deal. Looking to my right, I noticed that someone had shut the heavy wooden door behind us. We were inside and about to conduct business with the president of the United States. I couldn't help but cherish the moment.

Unlike his predecessor in office, President Bush was well known for being on time, if not early, in making his scheduled commitments. Today was no exception: We were seated and ready to go several minutes ahead of our scheduled briefing time.

While those in the media often sought to portray the president as being manipulated and led around by the vice president and other White House staff members, it didn't take me but a few seconds in Bush's presence to see his decisive leadership skills in action. From the outset, he immediately began by peppering Bridgeland about the progress we were making with his service initiative. Whom had we spoken to? What had they said? What were our next steps?

For one who was currently directing the nation's military as commander-in-chief in a war against terrorism, I was surprised by the scope and depth of the president's knowledge about the various community service programs. I knew he was covering material that we hadn't included in the president's briefing paper, as I had helped write the document in the first place. There was little doubt to anyone present that the one who was in charge and directing the course of our briefing was George W. Bush himself.

While the president received an update on our Peace Corps and Citizen Corps commitments, he seemed particularly interested in our progress in shopping the expansion of the AmeriCorps program on Capitol Hill. At this juncture, Bridge noted that we had been making great progress in our meetings with members of the House of Representatives and the Senate. It wasn't that I disagreed with Bridge's assessment; I just thought back to a tip I had always kept in the back of my mind before briefing the vice president: I was being paid not just for what I knew, but what I *thought*. Surely, the president's staff operated similarly. Why then, I asked myself, didn't Bridge elaborate a bit more clearly to the president that ironing out an agreement with conservatives in the House and the Senate for an AmeriCorps expansion bill would require a lot of time and effort on Bush's part. Real capital would have to be spent by the president, I thought, in order for his Call to Service to be successful.

That capital would have to be brokered in order to keep the House majority leader's promise to allow an AmeriCorps bill to reach the House floor for a vote. While Armey wouldn't hurt us directly, he clearly wasn't going to help us, either. Shouldn't the president know this early on? Shouldn't the president also be advised that Senator McCain had gently (but directly) criticized the president's decision not to go further in setting his service commitment goals for the AmeriCorps program?

Despite losing his run for the presidency, Senator McCain remained extremely popular with many different constituencies across the country. His popularity and level of stature could simply not be ignored. Yet,

Bridge characterized our meeting with McCain as a successful one. Shouldn't we share our thoughts a bit more candidly here?

Given that the president had created the USA Freedom Corps and highlighted our office during his State of the Union Address just a few months ago, surely he would put in the time to barnstorm the country and meet with members of Congress if we needed him to. I felt the president and his senior staff should have heard from us that we would need significant assistance from them to successfully move our legislative commitments ahead. But they wouldn't know if we didn't tell them, and this was our ideal opportunity to do so.

While Bridge had given the president a good overview of where we were, I felt that he could have gone several steps further by alerting the president about the potential storms ahead on Capitol Hill. Many conflicting thoughts went through my head as I pondered whether or not I should offer the president my thoughts. On the one hand, Bridge had been rather explicit in his instructions that I was to jump in if I could add context or information to our discussion. On the other hand, I didn't feel that these instructions meant that I could speak up and directly contradict an assessment given by my boss. After all, Bridgeland, not me, was an assistant to the president and a member of the president's senior staff. As a special assistant, I was two full levels below Bridgeland in the pecking order.

While I wanted to offer my thoughts in our initial discussion with the president, I wasn't sure what his reaction or the reaction of the other senior aides in the room would be. I decided that the better course of action would be to keep my thoughts to myself until Bridge and I had had the opportunity to discuss matters in private and in greater detail.

With the grandfather clock ticking loudly behind us, our time in the Oval was over seemingly as soon as it started. One of the president's most precious commodities is his limited time, and Chief of Staff Andy

Card zealously guards it. After the president had been briefed about our progress to date, Card said, "Thank you, Mr. President," as an indication that our briefing had come to a close.

As I stood to leave, the president smiled and gestured for me to draw near. I could hardly believe it when he stood up and put his arm around my shoulder. "You're doing a fine job," the president began. "I'm proud of you," he continued. I was stunned, but I managed to thank the president for his kind words. While I hadn't spoken a word during my first briefing with the president, I was trembling with excitement, eager for our next meeting. With the fear of the unknown behind me, I would step up and participate the next time, I promised myself. Hopefully, I wouldn't have to wait too long for another opportunity. At the same time, I was a bit worried about when we might see the president again to share our unvarnished thoughts as to the comments and impressions we had received upon Capitol Hill regarding his community service plans. Hopefully this was my nerves talking rather than a lurking suspicion that we had missed a choice opportunity to sound a warning that his beloved new Call to Service could be in jeopardy without proper use of the bully pulpit up on Capitol Hill. As I would discover in the weeks and months to follow, it would require a strenuous effort by senior staff and the president himself to keep the funding and interest levels for Bush's community service initiatives alive.

"Reposing Special Trust and Confidence"

Shortly after my first briefing with the president in the Oval Office, I arrived at my desk one day to find a simple document encased within a heavy frame at rest upon my chair. Grasping the frame on either side, I knew that my presidential commission had arrived. This document, affixed with the Great Seal of the United States and hand-signed by both the president and the secretary of state (the officer with authority to affix the seal), is one that has changed little since the early days of the Republic. In bold cursive script, the document proclaims for all to see:

George W. Bush
President of the United States of America
To Ronald Irvin Christie of California Greeting:

Reposing special trust and confidence in your Integrity, Prudence, and Ability: I do appoint you Special Assistant to the President and Director of Policy Initiatives and Government Affairs, authorizing you hereby to do and perform all such matters and things as to the said place or office do appertain,

or as may be duly given you in charge thereafter, and the said office to hold
and exercise during the pleasure of the President of the United States for the
time being.

In testimony whereof, I have caused the Seal of the United States to be here-
unto affixed.

Done at the City of Washington, this twenty fourth day of February, in the
year of our Lord two thousand two and of the Independence of the United
States of America the two hundred and twenty-sixth.

By the President, [signed] George W. Bush [and] Secretary of State Colin L.
Powell

This simple, yet powerful piece of paper felt heavy both in my hand
and in my mind. I had been officially authorized by the president of the
United States to undertake a position so that I could help implement his
budding community service initiative on behalf of the American people.
Thinking back to my meeting with Secretary Card before I was sworn
in I realized that this was not a job but an office that I was privileged to
hold only during the time and pleasure of the president's choosing. The
message and the warning were both unmistakable: I was to serve only as
long as the president felt I should serve. I wasn't entitled to my position,
nor did I have any claims of ownership should I decide to make a career
out of serving in the White House. No, I was there only as long as I got
the job done.

The solemn words of my commission as well as my first briefing of
the president led me to carefully and deliberately undertake my new
responsibilities. Whether I liked it or not, everywhere I went and in

every speech I gave, letter I wrote, or meeting I participated in, people would assume I had the power and the blessing of the president of the United States behind me.

This was immediately a sobering revelation. People weren't asking for my opinions or thoughts on Capitol Hill or around the country: They really wanted to know what the president's opinion was or what the president thought. Whether I actually knew what the president's opinion was or what he was thinking on a particular matter wasn't particularly relevant; I represented both his office and his administration before the public, and freelancing or careless speculation were simply not an option or luxury I could indulge in while in the public eye.

As we negotiated the AmeriCorps legislation on Capitol Hill or when I gave speeches around the country, senators and citizens alike would always ask me what the president thought about a particular topic or whether I agreed with a particular course of action he had taken. My response was always the same: "I don't speak for the president of the United States. Only he can do that." At the same time, I never doubted that when folks left a meeting with me or had walked away from one of my speeches, they would tell their friends or coworkers, "This is what Bush is thinking" or "Bush believes that . . ."

While working for both the vice president and president, I was honored to be invited by the White House Office of Public Liaison time and time again to serve as a surrogate speaker for the president and his administration beyond my duties at the USA Freedom Corps. From the frost of Augusta, Maine, to the summer heat of Jackson, Mississippi, I delivered remarks in more than a dozen states. Through all the civic groups, educators, politicians, and others before whom I had the privilege to represent the president, I had some of my most difficult moments speaking before audiences composed largely of African Americans.

As I was one of the few black officials in the White House, I felt an obligation to speak to groups composed of persons of color to do what I could to reinforce the impression that George W. Bush was the president of the United States for *all* Americans, regardless of their race, age, or political party affiliation. As I personally felt that the president's vision of reducing tax burdens while strengthening education and providing more access to healthcare would benefit all Americans in general and persons of color in particular, I leapt at the opportunity.

Perhaps I was naïve, but I thought I could relate and communicate with folks who might have been skeptical of the president and his administration but would be open to a fair and respectful opportunity to exchange opinions and ideas. For the most part, I was successful in reaching out and connecting with people. In particular, one of my favorite visits was to the Boys and Girls Club of Albany, New York, where the youngsters who were mostly black and Hispanic were thrilled to meet with someone who actually worked with the president of the United States.

These remarkable kids had cleaned up a polluted body of water and dug out a nature trail so that other children could enjoy the outdoors near the water. We all had a great time visiting with one another, and the adult mentors were thrilled to be able to thank the president through me for his dedication to the AmeriCorps program. I was equally impressed with their accomplishments and able to return to the White House and Capitol Hill to demonstrate with firsthand experience how the AmeriCorps program placed dedicated young men and women into the lives of impressionable youngsters from around the country.

For all the happy moments like my trip to Albany, though, I had more than my share of hostile treatment at the hands of African-American groups that invited me to speak to them. Sadly, one particular group comes to mind that bears mention. While I was still a member of the vice president's staff, I had the opportunity to speak before the National Black Caucus of Local Elected Officials (NBC-LEO). This group, an affiliate of the National League of Cities, was a body of black mayors, city council members, and state legislators. These leaders are charged to work for the best interests of African Americans due to their positions of responsibility, but I have never been so rudely received or treated during my nearly twelve years of public service as I was by this group.

Speaking before the NBC-LEO gathering in the Indian Treaty Room of the Old Executive Office Building, I went through a brief overview of the president's agenda during the fledgling days of his administration. Access to healthcare, reduction in taxes, and his No Child Left Behind education initiative were discussed, as well as the creation of the new Faith-Based and Community Initiatives Office at the White House. As I spoke, I was startled to see that a number of the members of the audience were shaking their heads as I spoke, waving their hands dismissively in my direction, or drowning out my speech by talking with their neighbors. I was almost literally at a loss for words: If people didn't want to hear about the president or his administration, why would they travel to Washington, come to the White House, and ask for a briefing from Public Liaison?

Rushing through my remarks so I could cede the floor and go back downstairs and get on with my day, I was approached by several members of the group who apologized for the poor behavior of their colleagues. This small group of mayors and legislators told me to keep my head up and ignore those who would mock me or show me disrespect because I was black and working for a Republican president. One man told me, "You're our Republican brother, and we need more people like you in here. Stay strong, hear?" I heard him and vowed to chalk up the rude behavior I had just seen as an aberration and not reflective of the group as a whole.

If only that assessment had proven correct. Nearly two years later, I received a frantic call from Public Liaison asking if I could pinch hit for them and deliver a set of remarks on the president's agenda at the last second. I had always teased my friend and former OPL Director Lezlee Westine that I worked for her, rather than for the USA Freedom Corps, given the number of speeches I had given for her office over the years. As my affection for Lezlee and my pride in representing the president before outside groups was well known, I happily accepted the opportunity to help out.

My heart sank, however, when I asked for the name of the group. "It's the National Black Caucus of Local Elected Officials," I was told. OPL knew of my treatment by the group previously, and they told me they understood if I wanted to decline. "No, I'll do it," I responded. So off I went to the Washington Hilton Hotel, infamously known as the location where would-be assassin John Hinckley Jr. nearly killed President Ronald Reagan years ago.

I arrived at the hotel and proceeded to the basement level where I would address the group in one of the smaller ballrooms. Entering the room, I was immediately welcomed to the podium and asked to deliver my remarks. I started by thanking the group for the invitation to speak, noting that it was nice to see them again after a few years. Launching into the heart of my remarks, I was stunned to hear booing and hissing as I discussed the president's faith-based initiative and other domestic policies. What was going on?

Continuing, I found the chorus of boos and catcalls getting louder and louder the longer I spoke. At this point, I stopped speaking altogether, and the gentleman who had introduced me implored his colleagues to treat me with respect and dignity. Stepping before the microphone once again, I tried to pick up my remarks from where I had left off. I vowed I would not let these rude people get the better of me. Perhaps there were folks in the audience who were receptive to my thoughts and would appreciate hearing what I had to say. Surely there were some friendly faces somewhere out there.

As I tried to wrap up, I could hardly hear myself speak. Hearing someone shout out that "George W. Bush doesn't give a damn about black folks, and you're just a sell-out fool" was too much for me. Snapping my folder shut and trying to maintain my composure by reminding myself that I represented the president in good moments and bad while outside the gates of the White House, I steadied myself. For the only time in my professional career, I told the group before me that I had come in friendship at their invitation to share the president's agenda and explore ways we could work together. Since they had shown such disrespect for me and the president, I could no longer continue, and I bid them good day. Then, things went completely out of control.

As I walked toward the edge of the stage, a number of men stood up and started screaming vulgar profanities at me. *Good God! Aren't these supposed to be leaders and pillars of their communities?* I thought to myself. As I arrived at the edge of the stage, a feeling I had never experienced before while on stage entered my mind: fear. Given the way I was being treated, I thought there was a chance someone might actually try to hurt me.

Backing up on the podium, I reached for my cell phone. Commissioned officers to the president are afforded the use of the White House motor pool to travel to and from official events. As I had left the White House to travel to the Hilton in my official capacity, I had called the motor pool for a lift. The drivers are senior noncommissioned officers of the United States Army and are as considerate as they are tough. At this moment, I needed a friendly face who could help get me out of there before things got any uglier.

Punching in the digits to call back to the White House, I really began to panic: I could not receive a signal to my cell phone. Now I didn't know what to do, and the obscenities continued to pelt me from every direction. As I pondered my next move, a small group of men and women approached the stage and motioned me forward.

Jumping off the stage, these kind folks surrounded me in a circle as I began walking toward the door that felt as if it were miles and miles away. As we walked toward the door, my protective circle was pushed this way and that as people actually jumped up to scream at me or get near me. This couldn't possibly be happening to me; this must be a bad dream.

Reaching the door, I burst through and began to run for the escalator at the end of the hall. A few of the legislators begged me to stop. I was a cauldron of emotions, shaking and barely able to keep my voice steady. As these kind people offered their profuse apologies and asked for my forgiveness, a few of the thugs that had frightened me inside had spilled outside the room. That was it; I was out of there.

Telling my rescuers that I held no ill will toward them, I rushed to the elevator and ran for the door. Thank goodness, the official black car I had arrived in was parked in the driveway. Yanking the door open, I threw my speech folder inside and slammed the door. I sat for a few moments and took several deep breaths. "Are you okay, sir?" the sergeant asked me with some concern. "I'm fine, Sarge," I replied. "Let's go home."

Home to the White House where I took such pride in my job and responsibilities, where I was treated with respect by my colleagues one and all, and away from a group of supposed black leaders who did nothing more than disgrace and dishonor the privilege of representing their fellow Americans in positions of responsibility.

President George W. Bush – Unplugged

MUCH HAS BEEN WRITTEN ABOUT THE 43RD PRESIDENT OF THE
United States thus far, yet relatively little has been written about what
George W. Bush is like as a man behind the scenes. My position at the
USA Freedom Corps gave me a unique opportunity to brief, interact
with, and observe the president up close on a number of occasions.
While often portrayed in the media as being manipulated by others and
devoid of intellect or warmth (or worse), the George W. Bush I had the
privilege to serve displayed none of these traits.

Instead, he was a highly organized and efficient man who expected the
best of himself and the staff around him. Pity the staffer who was insuf-
ficiently prepared to answer questions in their subject area of expertise;
the president didn't have the time or the patience to deal with sloppy
preparation, as I would observe on more than one occasion.

At the same time, the mainstream media's hostility toward the president often blinds them to a man who is extraordinarily loyal to his staff
and takes steps to reward those who are workhorses rather than show
horses. Even more surprising to me was the warmth the president displayed time and time again to those around him, including people he

had just met—not surprising in the sense that Bush is a kind and decent man, but surprising that with all the weight and responsibilities thrust upon him, the president is as decent and unaffected as anyone I have met in my day, a pleasant contrast to the arrogance and bravado one usually encounters in Washington D.C.

An early and amusing encounter I was fortunate to observe was when the president in the Oval Office subjected my boss, John Bridgeland, to teasing he would probably rather forget. Bridgeland, an extremely bright and capable lawyer educated at Harvard and the University of Virginia, was often known to wax poetic about philosophy and all matters intellectual to his friends and fellow staff members.

While I often enjoyed Bridge's history lessons and allegorical references, there were those in the White House whose patience for such digressions ran thin. It was Bridge's flair for the theatric that would subject him to a razzing by the president in the Oval Office.

We had gone in one day for one of our typical policy briefings to update the president on the status of his national and international community service initiative. As we walked over to the West Wing, Bridgeland, in a particularly chipper mood, had elaborated on some theory or another about Aristotle's Nicomachean ethics. Don't worry, I took a year of philosophy in college and didn't have the foggiest idea how this was apropos of anything. As he finished his comment, I begged Bridge not to bring up Aristotle or his theory on ethics before the president.

To my dismay, in the middle of Bridge's briefing, I watched, as if in slow motion, as he tried to explain Aristotle's theory of Nicomachean ethics. "What was that word, Bridge?" the president asked with a twinkle in his eye. "Is that one of those words you learned in Harvard?" the president continued. "Big word, Bridge." As the room erupted in laughter, the president had made his point with humor, but the lesson was as clear as day: Don't waste the president's time trying to impress him; just give him the facts he needs to know. While complex terms and SAT-like vocabulary might well be necessary to brief the president and his senior staff about certain topics, discussing the plight of young Americans in the AmeriCorps program didn't quite warrant channeling Aristotle.

Another lesson I learned, more poignant than the one above, is what happens when a member of the staff is unable to provide answers to straightforward questions posed by a pressed-for-time president of the United States. Given the enormous scheduling requests the president receives every year to deliver remarks to a wide variety of groups, he is simply unable to accommodate but a tiny fraction of those who seek a personal visit.

For some of the speech declines, the president deploys a surrogate—a member of the cabinet or White House official—to speak in his place. In limited circumstances, the president videotapes remarks to be broadcast before the audience that originally sought his in-person participation. While not nearly as exciting as having the president of the United States before them in person, taped remarks allow the president to interface with the group without declining their invitation outright or sending a surrogate in his place.

Approximately once a month, the president would set aside a block of time and record remarks for several groups in one sitting. On several occasions, Mr. Bush recorded remarks for community service venues, which those of us in the USA Freedom Corps would in turn provide to the organizations requesting his participation. After a few taping sessions, I realized that being in close proximity to the president and being unprepared to answer simple or relatively straightforward questions could subject one to a dressing down one would never forget.

2 December 2003. On this particular day, I found myself in the Map

Room on the ground floor of the White House residence. Originally used by President Franklin D. Roosevelt to monitor activities in World War II, it was set up for the current president of the United States to deliver his taped remarks. Unlike previous presidents, Mr. Bush was not fond of staff who liked to "hang around" in his presence. Either you had a job or purpose for being in the room, or you weren't there at all. As the Map Room was a rather small venue to begin with, there would only be a handful of aides present, other than the sound and light technicians.

As we waited on the president, who was wrapping up an event with NASCAR drivers on the South Lawn, I chatted with my colleagues who, like me, were on hand should the president have any questions about the remarks in their particular area of expertise. Israel Hernandez, righthand man to Senior Advisor Karl Rove was present, as was Kris Purcell from the Communications Office. We would also be joined by the president's personal aide, Blake Gottesman, and chief photographer, Eric Draper.

In all my time in the White House, I always found the arrival of the president to be akin to the calm before the storm. A room where chatter rang out suddenly grew silent as the president approached. A door would open, and the watchful eyes of the Secret Service would scan the room for potential threats before the door was closed once again. A few seconds later, the doorknob would turn with authority and the president of the United States would stride into the room.

Today was no exception to the rule. Those of us in the room who had been chatting amiably suddenly grew quiet. You could almost *feel* Bush coming. A few seconds later, the Secret Service did their brief visual and shut the door. Silence. Suddenly, the door to the Map Room swung open, and the president marched straight for the chair that had been set up for him before the camera and rows of lights. Here we go!

As we called out "Hello, Mr. President," Mr. Bush threw a wave in our general direction and said, "All right, guys, let's get this going." While I found the president to be a skillful off-the-cuff speaker, there were rumors I'd heard that sitting for tapings in a room devoid of a live audience was not one of the president's favorite activities. More to the point, the president much preferred to be talking to a group of real people rather than the eye of a camera lens.

That day, the president was to record four sets of remarks, three of which had been written by Brian Jones, a close friend of mine who served in Presidential Speechwriting. The last set of remarks had largely been written by me and John Bridgeland, which Speechwriting had polished up for us. With luck, the president wouldn't have any questions for any of us—he would zip through the various tapings, and we would all be on our respective ways. If only it was that easy.

Settling into his chair and performing audio checks, the president was ready to tape his first message. I believe we started off with a set of greetings for the USO and Armed Forces Entertainment, and Bush was nearly through the entire set of remarks before he stopped just short of the end. As he recorded again, Bush stopped to ask Dan Bartlett about something he had just read. "Why do we say that?" the president wanted to know. When he didn't have an immediate reply, the president dispatched Dan to find the answer while Bush skipped ahead to the next message.

Next, the president started reading remarks that had been prepared for the Iowa Farm Bureau Federation annual meeting. The president wasn't more than a few paragraphs into his remarks before he read, "That's why we eliminated the death tax so that farms and ranches stay in our families. By ending the unfair double taxation of income, we help Iowa's farmers and Iowa's small businesses, which are the engine of job creation."

A magnificent line, but for one little problem: The Congress had yet to pass legislation that eliminated the estate tax (or so-called death tax)

that applied to certain estates and small businesses. While the administration had long advocated a full repeal, Congress had only curbed the
estate tax on certain properties under a particular income threshold. The
line in the speech was not just inaccurate, it was flat-out wrong.

Whirling around in his chair, the president looked at me and said:
"Did you write this?" "No, sir," I immediately replied. Thank *God* I
hadn't. The president further asked me if we had eliminated the death
tax. "No, sir, Congress hasn't done that yet," I nervously replied. Talking
to himself as much as me, the president wanted to know why there was
a line in his speech touting an accomplishment that to date had not yet
taken place. Still, the president wanted to know who had written the
inaccurate line.

Flipping back to the end of the remarks, the president found what he
was looking for. At the end of most drafts of presidential remarks are the
name and phone number of the author, should someone in senior staff
have any questions or comments. This day, however, it wasn't a member
of the staff who had questions that needed an answer.

"Who in the heck is Brian C. Jones?" the president wanted to know.
Somehow this didn't seem to be the time to tell the president that Brian
and I had been friends for nearly a decade and that I had put in a strong
word with Speechwriting to help get him his job.

Fortunately for me, Israel Hernandez (or "Izzy" as we called him)
stepped up to the plate to take the heat for all of us. Izzy explained that
Brian had written the remarks for Karl's office and . . . But before Izzy
could finish, the president wanted to know why Brian had written that a
certain part of his tax plan had been written permanently into law when,
in fact, it hadn't. As Izzy struggled to respond, the president dispatched
Izzy to find out what had happened. Two staff down and counting.

About this point, I noticed that the president's personal aide and photographer had quietly removed themselves. With Bartlett and Hernandez gone, the small parameters of the Map Room seemed smaller still. Other than the technicians from the White House Communications Agency, Purcell and I were the only aides left in the room. This wasn't going the way anyone had planned it.

Moving ahead to the third set of remarks, which I believe was for the National Defense University Foundation American Patriot Award, I hoped that we would breeze through these and get to the USA Freedom Corps remarks. The president liked speaking about helping others and uniting the armies of compassion. At this point, I shuddered to think what would happen if the president had to stop his taping and ask another simple question that no one had the answer to.

This time, the president tightened his tie, looked into the camera lens, and prepared to begin again. Hardly more than a few seconds into the remarks, the president looked over at Purcell and asked him why something was phrased in a certain way. Uh-oh. Poor Kris had been standing a little bit in front of me, and he whirled around to consult his notes. Unfortunately for him, he collided with a light fixture that had been set in place to cast proper lighting upon the president. In slow motion, I watched both the light fixture falling and the look of panic on Kris's face as it began to fall down. I was close enough to catch it, but the president was not pleased. Exit, Mr. Purcell. And then there was one.

Now, I was the only one left from the original staff that had been able to provide answers to the president's questions. Asking the technicians to cue ahead to the next set of remarks, the ones that Bridgeland and I had written, the president cast a stern glance in my direction and offered me the following: "If there's anything wrong with this one, I'm not doing it, and I'm out of here. Do you understand me?" No pressure. None at all. "Yes sir, Mr. President."

After having fixed me with a long stare, the president turned back in his chair as the technical folks scrolled up to the remarks Bridge and I had put together. To say that my stomach was in knots was an understatement. Finally, the president began reading, and then he stopped. Turning to look at me once again, Bush shook his head and started from the top of the text and kept reading. As he read through to the end, I wanted to jump up for joy—he had done it and he didn't have any questions for me! Turning to look at me one more time, George W. Bush smiled at me and said, "That was good." As the color came back in my face and I started to breathe once more, I nodded and managed to squeak out, "Thank you, sir," before he turned back around and asked the tech wizards to scroll to an earlier speech.

Thankfully, my part of the exercise was over, and I retreated back to the wall, just under a map depicting Europe in World War II on the last day Roosevelt had used the room for that purpose: 3 April 1945. If the room had been originally used to chart the progress of a war, I felt that I had just dodged a serious bullet. In the days and weeks to follow, I would caution my colleagues while sitting at the staff table in the Mess what happens to the unfortunate staffer who has not fully scrubbed the drafts of the president's taped remarks for accuracy and clarity. Far from being disengaged and merely reading words from a teleprompter, President Bush displayed once again that he had paid strong attention to factual detail, and pity the staffer who didn't while in his presence.

And while the president can be extremely hard on his staff if they are unprepared, Mr. Bush possesses a warmth and true love of people that the press has elected to largely ignore.

On 5 February 2004, the president flew to Charleston, South Carolina, to deliver remarks on his administration's efforts to protect Americans by strengthening our port security. As my mother was living in Charleston at the time, I called the president's Advance team to see if I could arrange a meeting between the president and my mom—perhaps out at Air Force One. While they were unable to arrange that meeting, Advance offered to place my mother at the head of the rope line, just in front of where Mr. Bush would be speaking. Perhaps when he finished his comments, the president would work the rope line and say a few words to my mother.

Thrilled by the prospect of meeting the president, my mother arrived at the venue hours ahead of time to stake out her spot. As time passed, dozens and dozens of people arrived to claim a choice spot, but my mother had already snared one at the head of the rope line where she couldn't be missed. Besides a book she had brought to pass the time, my mother had brought a picture of me from a briefing I had done in the Oval Office just prior to the president signing legislation into law that would create the African-American Museum of History and Culture. My mom wanted the president to autograph the photo for her, and she was bound and determined to get it signed.

Sure enough, as the president concluded his remarks, Mr. Bush walked from the stage and began to shake the hands of those who had gathered along the rope line. Sensing her chance, my mom had the picture of me and the president out, patiently waiting for him to get there.

Just prior to the president's arrival at her spot in the rope line, the Secret Service noted that my mother had a pen and picture at the ready. "Put that away, ma'am; he's not going to sign anything today," the agent told her. "Wait a minute," he continued. "That's Ron, isn't it?"

"Yes," my mother replied. "That's my son." As the agent walked past, the president stopped right in front of my mother. "Is that for me? Can I have it?" he asked. In a response only a mother could get away with, she said, "No, but you can sign it." As the president peered down at the photograph in his hand, he realized who the two people in the photograph were. "Hey, that's Ron Christie," he exclaimed. "I know," my mom said. "He's my son."

According to my mother, the president leaned over and put his arm around her and said, "Your son is doing a great job, and I'm real proud of him. He's a good man." The president then reached for a pen to sign the photograph as my mother had hoped. But that wasn't the only gift he would leave her with that day. Just as he was about to walk away and greet the other guests on the rope line, the president of the United States drew close to my mother and gave her a peck on the cheek. "Nice to meet you, ma'am, and I'm really proud of your son."

A few weeks later, I was sitting in my office when the phone began to ring. When I looked at the caller ID, I noticed it was Blake Gottesman, the president's personal aide. While we were very friendly with one another, Blake had never called me on the phone before.

Cutting right to the chase, Blake wanted to know how my mother spelled her name. "M-A-T-T-I-E Christie," I replied. "Why?" Blake responded that the president had a photograph of himself and my mother, and he wanted to sign it. I couldn't believe it: After an event that had taken place several weeks earlier, the president thought enough to take a few moments out of his busy schedule to sign a photograph of him greeting my mother. I was touched and told Blake to thank the president for me.

I couldn't help but think that Bush was doing nothing more than taking a moment to make a mother who was already proud of her son even prouder. Now my mother had her own picture with the president for the entire world to see. One small act of kindness on the president's part, but one giant sense of pride for my mother that has led to a lifetime of gratitude from my family.

Even more gratifying for me to witness up close, however, was the level of generosity and kindness the president and the first lady bestowed upon a group of small children and their families during the Christmas holiday season in 2003. The White House Office of Public Liaison asked if I could work with them to put together a holiday event for the president and first lady to participate in to celebrate the season with those who were less fortunate. Associate Director of OPL Matthew Smith and I settled on visiting the Shiloh Baptist Church in Alexandria, Virginia, for the president and Mrs. Bush to participate in the church's angel tree program. This was a program for children who had one or both of their parents in prison who might otherwise have a bleak holiday without any gifts under the tree.

Concerned members of the community could elect to purchase gifts for the needy children to ensure that Santa Claus would pay them a visit and leave behind toys and gifts from his sleigh. This year, as in years past, the White House staff had been actively involved in buying Barbie dolls, action figures, and a wide variety of toys for the children. Unlike years past, however, a group of children would get to meet the president and Mrs. Bush and receive something more important than a gift.

The plan was to have the Bushes arrive at the Shiloh Baptist Church, exchange a few gifts with the children, and then depart once every child had received a gift. Having seen the president melt in front of little kids in numerous events before, I knew that we would be in for something special that day. As Matt Smith, the other co-lead for the event, had to be out of town, I would accompany the president and Mrs. Bush in the motorcade and be on hand if they should need anything. The reality of the situation was that I would be a spectator to an amazing display of kindness and compassion that never finds its way into the headlines or other media coverage of the president.

Roaring out of the gates near the South Lawn of the White House, our motorcade traveled through Washington D.C. before racing onto Interstate 295 toward the Woodrow Wilson Bridge that spans the Potomac River and separates the states of Maryland and Virginia. As we zipped along the highway, I couldn't help but imagine the shock our fellow commuters must have felt when they saw a small armada of police motorcycles and other vehicles followed by a black limousine carrying the president of the United States fly by with the American flags flapping.

Across the Woodrow Wilson Bridge and into Alexandria, our motorcade swung smartly into slots before the church, and out we went. Along with Deputy Press Secretary Trent Duffy, Advance man Steve Atkiss, and photographer Tina Hager, we swung open the doors of our van and ran into the church with the president and the first lady.

As we entered, a small group of children stood in a corner of the room singing Christmas carols. The rear door of the church swung open, and the traveling press pool pushed and jostled into position to take shots of the president and first lady once they arrived. The press wouldn't have to wait long. Moments later, a beaming George and Laura Bush emerged from a side door and walked out to greet the children. As the lights flashed and the cameras whirred into action, the president put his prepared remarks into his jacket pocket and spoke warmly about the Christmas season to the children.

Following his remarks, the president and first lady handed out presents to several of the children as called for in our Advance preparations. At this juncture, the press pool was escorted out of the room, and so I figured the end of the event had come just as quickly as it had started. It turns out I was wrong and in a terribly good way.

The president and the first lady stood before the group of proud mothers and fathers, aunts and uncles, grandmothers and grandfathers, and other loved ones as they deviated from the original plans and dispensed gifts to each and every child in the room. Just watching the children with eyes as wide as saucers reach up to receive a Christmas gift from the president and Mrs. Bush followed by a tiny, "Thank you, Mr. President, thank you, Mrs. Bush" brought tears to my eyes.

But the first family wasn't finished; they were just getting started. After every child had received his or her gift, the president asked if anyone wanted their picture taken. I was stunned to watch young and old alike flock to the president. What surprised me was that to the last, each and every person wanted to hug Mr. Bush and his wife. One excited woman announced to no one in particular, "We love you, George Bush." This from a group of urban churchgoers whose congregation that day was 100 percent black. Young and old, I was touched to see that the president and the first lady had handed out more than gifts that afternoon— they had also handed out a little bit of themselves and a lot of love in the process. The sincerity and genuine admiration shown by all in the room was something that plays time and time again in my mind to this day.

After all the hands had been shaken, gifts taken, and hugs given, the president and Mrs. Bush prepared to walk from the room and head to the motorcade to return to the White House. Catching my eye, the president grinned at me and waved. Shaking my head and smiling right back, I returned his wave and turned to race back to the motorcade. Settling back in the staff van, I thought back to a line that the president had uttered in the State of the Union Address the year before that best summed up what I had seen: "And through the momentum of millions of acts of kindness and decency, we will rebuild America one heart and one soul at a time." One heart and one soul at a time. That day the president exercised two of the most powerful tools in his arsenal to impact the lives of the Americans before him: love and compassion. This is a side of George W. Bush that relatively few have seen and hardly anyone has taken the time to write about. Behind closed doors and away from the glare of the media's lights, the commander-in-chief and president of the United States is a genuinely warm and compassionate person who loves regular people. Contrary to the harsh criticism one often reads about the president by people who have never met him, I can't help but set the record straight. In a word, the president is a pretty cool guy, and I know more than a dozen children in Alexandria, Virginia, will back me up without a moment's hesitation.

Karl Rove:
The Real McCoy

FROM THE OUTSIDE LOOKING IN, KARL ROVE MUST SEEM TO be a political figure who is larger than life. Hailed by the president himself as the architect of his successful reelection to the White House, Rove has had more laudatory phrases thrown his way than any single staff member of Bush's team, with the possible exception of Karen Hughes. "Boy Genius." "Bush's Brain."

Watching the Karl Rove figure on television during the 2000 presidential campaign, I thought all the accolades and praise heaped on one man was a bit of an exaggeration. One person can't be that talented, I thought to myself time and time again.

Yet from the inside of the White House complex, I had the opportunity to work and interact with the Karl Rove upon which the media spotlight has never shined. This is the man who understands the history of the presidency better than most scholars, a man who has successfully merged policy wonk intellect with a wicked sense of humor, and a man who is beloved by nearly everyone in the White House, from the stewards in the White House Mess to his colleagues on the president's senior staff. Little did I know what Karl Rove would mean to my personal and professional development during my time in the White House.

Beyond working with Rove in the Conspiracy of Deputies, I would run into him time and time again in various policy meetings while I was on the staff of the vice president and the president. One memorable moment comes to mind early in my tenure in the White House.

One morning, I arrived in the office of then White House economic advisor Dr. Larry Lindsey for a senior-level meeting Cesar had asked me to cover for him. From my early days on Cheney's staff, Mary Matalin had been teasing me about my large "Coke bottle" glasses that she had announced, to no one in particular, made me look like, in her words, "a big geek." While her remarks were not meant to hurt me personally, Matalin continued by saying that I should invest in a pair of contact lenses so the world would be able to see my face. Given that Matalin had once called me the son she had never had during a joint speech we had given before a group of young students called "Freedom's Answer," I was willing to cut Matalin all the slack in the world. I eventually caved and started wearing contacts.

The morning I showed up to Lindsey's office for the policy meeting, I was more than a little surprised to see Rove sitting at the table with then Secretary of the Treasury Paul O'Neill and Labor Secretary Elaine Chao. This was clearly more than just "some policy meeting" that Cesar had asked me to cover.

As I moved toward the table to join the group, I heard Rove's voice from across the room: "What do you think? I like Ron better with his glasses on than his contacts." "I don't know," Chao replied. "I like how he looks." For his part, O'Neill was nodding his head in agreement with his fellow member of the president's cabinet.

Up to this point, I had seen Karl here and there in the hallway or around the table during Conspiracy of Deputies meetings. This was the first time he referred to me by name, let alone discussed me in my presence with two members of the cabinet. This from the man who was thought by many to be the most powerful man in the White House other than the VP?

If the meeting that day showed me anything, it was that Karl was just getting started with teasing me and having a good time at my expense. Later that year, I had heard that Rove and I would both be attending a fundraiser for then Virginia Attorney General Mark Early, who was running for the Governor's Mansion in Richmond. On a whim, I asked Susan Ralston, Karl's executive assistant and virtual right hand at the time, if Karl was driving over to the event. Not only was Karl driving to the event, she said, but I was free to catch a ride with him if I wanted.

Meeting up at the senior staff parking lot on West Executive Drive, Rove and I walked over to his vehicle to head to the Early fundraiser. When we arrived at his car, I couldn't resist a dig of my own: "You drive a Jaguar? Isn't that a foreign car?" In a parking lot populated with a wide assortment of American cars, I was shocked that the president's senior advisor would roll around town in an English car.

Without skipping a beat, Rove looked at me and smiled: "Jaguar's owned by Ford. This is an American car, baby!" Slipping into the front seat, I had no idea what I had gotten myself into. Simply put, Karl drives like he talks, which is fast and spirited. Unfortunately, Karl is also one of the types of people who maintains eye contact with you while he speaks. Not at all a problem when you're seated next to him in a chair or across the table during lunch at the Mess. But when you're riding with Mr. Rove, and he maintains the same level of eye contact, you can be in for the ride of your life.

I felt as if I were on the soundstage from some old Hollywood movie set where one character drives the car and the other frantically tries to get his driving companion's focus back on the road before the car crashes in a huge fireball. I wish I could tell you what we discussed that day, but I have no idea. While awed to be in Rove's presence, I was praying we wouldn't end up wrapped around a lamppost at the side of the road.

Once we arrived at the event at the foot of Capitol Hill, I was relieved to have both feet back on solid ground. Upon entering the event, Rove was immediately flocked by the candidate running for office as well as the supporters who had shown up to get a glimpse of Karl. Reverting back to my staffer mind-set from my days on Capitol Hill, I thought that I would fade into the background as Rove worked the room, but he was not cooperating.

As he shook hands with person after person, Karl made sure to introduce me by name and with a kind word. This is but one of many reasons why Karl is so well-liked on the White House staff: In situations where it would be easy for him to bask in the glory of his remarkable accomplishments, he goes out of his way to praise the work and abilities of others rather than his own.

As I transitioned over to the president's staff in early 2002, I would discover time and again that Karl the prankster could show up unannounced and have a room in stitches at a moment's notice. I've lost count of the number of times where I was seated in the Mess for lunch and heard that unmistakable cackle of laughter from across the room. I'd look across the room to see Rove take a water pitcher from the hands of a Navy steward and refill the glasses of startled patrons. You could hear the unasked question hanging in the air: "*Isn't that Karl Rove? Filling up water glasses?*"

One of my favorite events took place in the Mess with Karl just prior to my departure from the White House. I had taken my parents and my fiancée to the Mess just days prior to leaving the president's staff, and I had asked Rove to say a few words to my parents if he had the time.

Just after Andy Card had come over to shake hands and tell my parents how proud he was of me for my work in the White House, Rove came over for a few words of his own. After introducing himself to my folks and my bride-to-be, Rove loudly announced: "We just *love* your son here in the White House." After a pause, Rove reflected and then added: "But we love Ron in an appropriate kind of way."

Rove's theatrics had even made their way into the Oval Office itself. Once, Bridgeland and I were briefing the president on the latest progress with his Citizen Corps initiative when the president sharply cut Bridgeland off to ask Karl what he was doing. "Reading a book, sir" was his response. Who other than Karl Rove could tease the president of the United States while reading a book in the Oval Office during a domestic policy briefing? Rove wasn't finished, however. Holding up the book in his hand, it was the Molly Ivins book called *Shrub* that was highly critical of the president. "Put that away, Karl," the president said with a smile. The entire room erupted in laughter. The president, Andy Card, everyone. Rove's sense of humor was truly infectious, and you couldn't help but laugh in his presence.

At the same time, Rove's contagious humor belied a man who was a serious student of history and well versed in policy matters. Shortly after the September 11 attacks, Karl directed his Office of Strategic Initiatives to create a lecture series entitled "Man in the Arena." These lectures were designed to teach mid- and senior-level White House staff about key events in American and world history and how they related to us in the post-9/11 world. Rove brought in distinguished authors and historians to read from their works and then relate them to the dangerous world we now lived in.

One of the earliest lectures I attended involved the noted historian

Edmund Morris. Morris is the Pulitzer Prize-winning author of the biography series chronicling the life of President Theodore Roosevelt. The work, entitled *Theodore Rex*, discussed the span of Roosevelt's life as he entered the White House as president of the United States following the assassination of President McKinley in Buffalo, New York.

Morris challenged us to reflect on the times before us as well as those before the White House staff of President Roosevelt. Both presidents had come to power at the turn of the century following a violent event that had transformed the consciousness of the American people: the murder of the president of the United States in 1901 and the terrorist attacks upon America in 2001. We were told that while these were turbulent times, we should keep our wits and bearings about us as the president needed our heads to be clear and our advice sound.

At the end of the day, I found Rove to be focused on one thing and one thing only: doing whatever it took to advance the agenda of President George W. Bush. Whether that meant keeping the staff loose through his jokes or contemplative about their jobs and responsibilities in this unique period in American history, Rove understood his role as the senior advisor inside and out. For the nearly three and a half years I served in the White House, I saw Rove perform both duties flawlessly, up close and personal. The nation and the president are well-served with Karl Rove on the job.

Our Eye on America – Senior Staff

7:28 AM. AS THE HEAVY METAL BARRIER LOWERED INTO THE ground at the Jackson Place parking lot just across the street from the White House, I raced my car to the far end of the lot, as I did most mornings, and parked as close as possible to Pennsylvania Avenue.

Charging out the door and across the street to the Northwest Gate of the White House, I could hear the buzz of the electric lock being released, so I could push open the gate without breaking stride. "Running late, sir?" the Secret Service agent always asked. "Don't you know it," I always replied while my briefcase was being run through the x-ray machine and I entered my code in the keypad.

7:29 AM. After bidding the Secret Service farewell, I cleared the guard booth and quickly hastened up the path of the North Lawn of the White House. To my right most mornings, the television lights blazed and lit up the early morning sky as well-known White House correspondents prepared to report to the nation from their reserved patch of rubble called "Pebble Beach." Rushing more quickly still down the path, I would always speed-dial my then-fiancée to let her know that I had made it and to tell her I loved her. I'm sure that more than once the viewers of *The Today Show* saw a rapidly scurrying figure rush by with a cell phone in hand as Campbell Brown bantered back and forth with Katie and Matt.

Almost there. As I reached the white columns just outside of the West Wing Reception Room, the Marine sentry on duty would crisply open the door and stand at attention, holding the door as I rushed through. Did I make it? Shedding my outer coat in an anteroom, I headed left and looked at the door of the Roosevelt Room. If it was still open, I still had a chance.

Through the open door now, I aimed for my seat on the couch opposite the round table in the middle of the room. To my left, the portrait of Theodore Roosevelt gazed down upon me as he sat astride his rearing horse. Across from my vantage point was a heavy wooden door with a brass handle—the Oval Office lay steps away on the other side. Adjacent to the door was the dark blue flag with the seal of the president of the United States.

Around me, Senior Advisor Karl Rove, National Security Advisor Condi Rice, and Press Secretary Ari Fleischer (and later Scott McClellan), among others, would take their seats. At 7:30 AM on the dot, Chief of Staff Andy Card would enter the room and pull yet another heavy wooden door shut and call out for the president's scheduler to outline the president's day, minute by minute. Conversations ceased immediately, and another meeting of the president's senior staff was called into order.

Like clockwork, while much of official Washington remains at home reading the paper or drinking coffee, approximately twenty-five people gather in the president's conference room every morning to participate in one of the most influential meetings in the world. Fortunately, my boss sent me in his place to senior staff more often than not during the week, and I was given a rare glimpse into how the president's most senior advisors deliberate the issues of the day.

This ritual is the one opportunity each day where nearly all of the president's senior advisors are in the same place at the same time. Chief of Staff Andy Card presides over the gathering and makes the most of the thirty minutes or so when he has their full time and attention.

Without exception, the meeting begins in the same manner every morning. Placed upon each chair in the room is a miniature copy of the president's schedule upon a heavy white card embossed with "The White House" at the top. As Card brings the meeting to order, the president's director of scheduling and appointments calls out the various engagements and meetings the president will conduct, regardless of where he is in the world. I've heard discussions about meetings with the queen of England, the prime minister of Israel, and the Super Bowl champion New England Patriots. If the president has a meeting that bears discussion by a member of his senior staff, that discussion occurs here.

After the scheduler finishes the rundown of the president's activities for the day, the White House press secretary is up to provide his colleagues a breakdown of news that took place overnight as well as events and activities that are likely to generate news during that particular day. At times, this could be a tense discussion as reports of American servicemen who perished while serving their country or other sad news are brought to the attention of the group.

Next up, the director of the White House Legislative Affairs Office is called upon to report on what took place in the House of Representatives and the Senate the day before. These were often fascinating discussions as the priorities of the congressional leaders and the president did not always coincide. Members of Congress love to spend money and send projects back to their districts, and the president and his Budget Office were always trying to hold the line on spending. Oftentimes former Budget Director (and current Governor of Indiana) Mitch Daniels or current chief Josh Bolten would chime in on these reports with a discussion of what the president's bottom line or spending priority was for the particular program or project in question. There was always the push of Congress for more spending, juxtaposed with the firm hand of the director of the Office of Management and Budget laying down the gauntlet regarding what the president had proposed to spend on the program in his budget.

I never envied Mitch or Josh their respective positions as they were always the ones putting themselves between the president and the members of Congress to say "Not so fast" to those who wanted to spend money as if it grew on trees, while preserving the president's relationship with the member of Congress in question. After all, it was a member of the president's staff, rather than the president himself, who was sent to the Hill to be the bearer of bad news. Not the easiest position to be in, for certain.

Continuing around the table, the next report was given by the national security advisor. Dr. Rice was usually with the president during senior staff, and her deputy (and current national security advisor, Steve Hadley) would alert his colleagues to important meetings or progress with foreign leaders from around the globe. In the days immediately following the 9/11 attacks, these reports were particularly enlightening as the condolences expressed or the offers of help extended from around the world were fascinating to hear.

At this point, it was time for the report from the senior advisor. While senior staff meetings were generally formal and efficient, Karl Rove had a way of lightening things up and making the session more interesting. One time I arrived in the Roosevelt Room to find a single sheet of paper on it that said, "If Karl Were Chief of Staff for the Day." Beneath this heading were several coffee drink choices one could check off for Karl's staff to supposedly hand-deliver. But while Karl could be the one dispensing the humor in senior staff, on more than one occasion, I had seen someone poke fun at Rove for our amusement.

One morning, I showed up and took my seat on the couch in the Roosevelt Room just across the table from Andy Card. As I glanced at the president's schedule and flipped through the press clips from the night before, I spied another sheet of paper in my stack. An anonymous member of senior staff had found an old picture from Karl's College Republican days and distributed it for all to see. What we saw was, putting it delicately, a pencil-pushing Rove with enormous glasses and an unruly mop of hair on his head. And was that a pocket protector?

When Rove entered the room, there was a smattering of snickering as we waited to see how long it would take him to discover the prank. Fortunately, Karl took it as well as he dished it out, and he held up the picture and laughed along with the rest of us.

After Karl, Card would ask if then Communications Director Karen Hughes, former White House Counsel Alberto Gonzalez, or the homeland security advisor had any points they wanted to add. If not, Card would scan the room looking for either anyone he hadn't called on or to see if anyone had anything they wanted to add. About half the time I was there, Andy would run around the table before calling out: "Freedom Corps. Ron Christie. Anything?" More often than not, I would decline to add anything, but if our office had a presidential event or brief in the Oval Office that day, I would share that with my colleagues.

Generally, once Card made it to me, senior staff was winding to a close. Always respectful of other people's time, Card tried to wind the meeting down as close to eight o'clock as possible. At that point, we would all scatter away to carry out our respective tasks.

I was privy to some fascinating discussions about events that will reverberate long after President Bush's second term in office has ended.

I was there the morning after the president landed on the deck of the USS *Abraham Lincoln* and infamously spoke before a gathering of sailors in front of a banner that read, "Mission Accomplished." I was also there just after the space shuttle *Columbia* tragically exploded, killing all the astronauts aboard. All in all, I was privileged to share this rare view in the White House as senior advisors discussed, argued, and poked fun at one another as they sought to provide the best counsel to the president of the United States.

Inside the Cabinet

WHILE CHIEF OF STAFF ANDY CARD PULLS TOGETHER HIS senior staff every morning to discuss the issues of the day, the president of the United States convenes his cabinet approximately once every forty-five days and receives a report on what his administration is doing on behalf of the American people. On 2 February 2004, I was privileged to join the president and his cabinet for their first gathering of the new year.

Unlike senior staff meetings, where a number of deputy assistants to the president are invited to participate, cabinet meetings are even more selective and hierarchal—only the dozen or so assistants to the president, the most senior of the president's staff, are invited to attend. While I had assumed the helm of the USA Freedom Corps office as acting director with Bridge's resignation and departure the previous December, I was surprised that Andy Card and Deputy Chief of Staff Harriet Miers (as of this writing, Supreme Court nominee) treated me with much the same deference afforded to Bridge as an assistant to the president, evidenced by the phone call I received in late January to confirm my attendance and participation in the cabinet meeting. "Are you kidding me?" I responded to the assistant from the chief of staff's office.

"Andy and Harriet would like you to be there if you can make it," I was told. Hmmm, could I fit it in my busy schedule to join the president and his cabinet to discuss the course of his administration for 2004? Somehow I thought I could make the time. I could hardly wait.

That morning, I made my way to the West Wing to attend the gathering of the cabinet. While being in the presence of the president was always a thrill (with the possible exception of various tapings in the Map Room), I was even more excited than usual to see what went on in the room with the doors closed and cameras absent. Walking into the West Lobby, I greeted my friend Ann Gray (then the West Wing receptionist and now the White House intern coordinator) and told her of my excitement to join the meeting. "Have fun and good luck," she called out as I turned left past the Roosevelt and headed to the Cabinet Room just adjacent to the Oval Office.

This room overlooking the Rose Garden was added during President Theodore Roosevelt's expansion of the West Wing in 1902. In the middle of the room sits a large mahogany conference table, which was a gift from President Richard Nixon back in 1970. The table sits upon a sturdy green rug with gold and green borders. Taking in the room, I felt like a tourist and recalled my family's nickname for me: Forrest Gump.

Unlike most other rooms in the West Wing, the Cabinet Room is strictly off limits to staff, and only the president of the United States can convene a meeting inside with his cabinet or congressional or military leaders. Given the closely guarded access to the room and that this was my first cabinet meeting, I wasn't sure where to go or what to do.

Fortunately, my good friend Tevi Troy was on hand to show me the ropes. Tevi served as special assistant to the president and deputy cabinet secretary (and currently as the president's deputy domestic policy advisor). The Office of Cabinet Affairs was responsible for coordinating activities of the various executive branch agencies as well as pulling the members of the cabinet together to meet with the president. A veteran attendee of cabinet meetings, Tevi guided me along the wall just behind the large table in the middle of room to my seat.

Adorning my chair was a heavy card with the presidential seal embossed in gold with "Mr. Christie" etched in fancy black calligraphy. "This is you," Tevi said. With a pat on my shoulder, he went back to his post at the head of the room and checked off cabinet secretaries from his list as they arrived, much like a teacher calling roll with an attendance sheet.

From my vantage point, the scene looked like a high school student council meeting, except that the participants here were all decked out in expensive business suits. Just in front of me there was Secretary of State Colin Powell exchanging laughs with National Security Advisor Condi Rice in one corner. Just a few feet away, there was Secretary of Defense Don Rumsfeld holding court with Commerce Secretary Don Evans and several others. Watching the most powerful men and women in America catch up with one another was a surreal experience.

Even more interesting for me was how each and every seat in the room and around the table had been assigned due to strict seniority. In the center of the table on the east side of the room sat a chair that was slightly taller than the rest. This, of course, would be the seat occupied by the president of the United States. Vice President Cheney's chair sits directly opposite the president's.

The secretary of state, as the most senior member of the cabinet, sits directly to the president's right, and the secretary of the treasury, ranking second, sits to the vice president's right. So on and so forth around the room, the members of the cabinet are arranged.

As I tried to figure out who would sit where, a few of the cabinet members I had interacted with during my time in the White House graciously took a moment to say hello. Secretary Powell, always friendly to me, said hello, as did Secretary of Labor Elaine Chao (behind whom I was seated) and Secretary Evans.

At this point, the vice president entered the room, and the cheerful conversations ringing out around the room immediately grew quiet. I was surprised by the reaction of the cabinet secretaries to Cheney's arrival. A glance at my watch told me it was nearly show time. I had just taken my seat when my former boss and VP Chief of Staff Scooter Libby leaned over to tell me to stay standing until the president had entered the room. Good ol' Scooter, I thought. Still looking after me nearly two years to the day after I left the vice president's office.

Abruptly, the door in the back of the room opened and President George W. Bush strode in. Immediately upon his arrival, the room was quiet as a tomb. "Please be seated," the president formally told one and all. As we took our seats, the president continued, "Mr. Vice President, I believe you have a prayer for us?" "Yes, Mr. President, I do," Cheney replied.

With our heads bowed, we listened to the vice president deliver a heartfelt prayer in which he asked the Lord to watch out for us, but to particularly watch over the brave men and women in America's armed forces who were protecting us all. I had never seen the spiritual side of the vice president before, and I was struck by how much comfort and conviction came through his voice as he spoke.

With the prayer concluded, the president immediately took the floor and firmly told his cabinet what his expectations were of them for the coming year. In a presentation that lasted about ten minutes, the president reminded his cabinet that while this was an election year, their job was to do the job of the American people and nothing more. The campaigning, once it began in earnest for the president's second term, would be done by the president and the vice president. The president continued by noting that he would make the case to the American people about the importance of the continuing war against terrorism in general and the stakes for success on the battlefield in Iraq in particular.

The president's instructions and expectations to his cabinet were nothing short of mesmerizing. Every set of eyes and ears in the room were transfixed and hanging on the president's every word. In a calm yet commanding voice, the president made it very clear to everyone present that they needed to keep their focus and priorities on their particular job rather than worrying about the complexities of the war in Iraq or the daunting road ahead for the president's reelection (which at that moment, looked like it would be tight, down to the last vote counted).

After the president finished his remarks, he turned to Secretary of State Colin Powell for a rundown on what was going on in the world. Much has been written in the media about the supposed tensions between the president and his former secretary of state. From my vantage point not ten feet away, the respect and affection between the two men was palpable and genuine. Before Powell started his remarks, the president said repeatedly, "Man, I'm glad you're here; we need you." As the meeting progressed and Powell concluded his remarks, I watched as the two men sitting side by side passed notes back and forth like two high school buddies.

After Powell finished his comments about American diplomatic efforts around the world, Secretary of Defense Donald Rumsfeld took the floor to provide the president and his colleagues with an update on the war against terrorism. You can appreciate why I will not delve into detail regarding Secretary Powell and Secretary Rumsfeld's status reports, but both men spoke knowledgeably and confidently about both the progress that had been made as well as the challenges America and her allies would face in the days ahead.

Without warning, the president turned in his chair and called upon Secretary of Labor Elaine Chao. Our printed itinerary did not list a report by Chao, and sitting right behind her, I saw her shoulders tense up as the president called out to her, "Elaine, you just got back from Iraq. Give us a report on what you saw." From the few meetings I had attended with her, I had always found Secretary Chao to be extremely organized and thorough. I also liked her personally, as she always made time to speak to me whenever our paths crossed. Yet, judging from her reaction that day, she looked like the rest of us when called on unexpectedly by the president: a little tense and a little nervous. Whether one was a special assistant to the president like me or a full-blown cabinet secretary, George W. Bush has a commanding aura of authority, and no one serving in his administration wants to appear uninformed or worse in the presence of the president or their colleagues.

After the secretary of labor gave the president and her colleagues a report on her successful trip to the Iraqi theatre of operations, the president called on several more cabinet secretaries before he was through. After thanking everyone present for their hard work and service to the country, the president announced that unless anyone had any questions of him, he was ready to let the press into the room for an on-camera report of the cabinet meeting that had just been held.

For all my years of working in the White House and observing the media do their job as the president did his, I was thoroughly unprepared for what happened next. As soon as the doors to the Cabinet Room opened, a horde of reporters and photographers poured in, followed by audio and video technicians. Where the room had been totally silent but for the president's voice not a few moments before, now people were pushing, shoving, and jostling to get into position before the president.

A couple of microphone boom operators nearly took my head off as they held out their microphones across the table.

For his part, the president calmly watched the scene of utter chaos unfold around him. Once the jostling and jockeying drew to a close, the president shared with the press and the American people his impressions of the meeting we had just concluded. People always say the president looks uncomfortable or unsure of himself in front of the television camera lens. From where I sat, I was amazed he was even speaking at all. The intensity of the television lights was nearly blinding, and they weren't even directed at me. With the booms extended near his face and the clicks of the photographers nearly deafening as he spoke, I was amazed the president could concentrate, let alone calmly articulate a synopsis of what had just taken place with his cabinet.

After issuing a report and answering a few questions, thankfully the press was led out of the room. As the president rose to his feet, we all stood. Although no one said as much, it was obvious the meeting was over. As no one told me I had to leave, I decided to loiter near my seat to see what would happen next. I was surprised to watch a few well-known members of the cabinet push their way over to where the president was standing.

Delicately, I wondered if these folks, not accustomed to seeing the president as often as the secretary of state or defense, for example, were making the most of their opportunity to talk to or be photographed with the president. As there is always a White House photographer around to capture nearly every step the president makes, they are also in a position to capture a particular member of the cabinet as they speak to Mr. Bush, a moment in time which would shortly arrive to that particular secretary as a lovely photograph suitable for framing.

I marveled at the scene of former lawyers, businessmen, and captains of industry who were now members of the cabinet, asserting themselves to get near the president. The scene made me chuckle: outside of the room, the group of senior leaders of our government projected a strong, confident image for the entire world to see. Inside the Cabinet Room, they were as mortal, nervous, and thrilled to be near the president of the United States as the most junior member of the White House staff.

After the last photograph had been taken and the last hand shaken, the president scanned the room one last time before he walked back to the Oval Office. As was his custom when he saw me from afar, the president smiled broadly at me and threw a hearty wave in my direction. And then he was gone.

A Portrait of Courage

ON THE AFTERNOON OF 21 JANUARY 2002, I WAS HONORED TO be in the East Room of the White House for a celebration to commemorate the Dr. Martin Luther King Federal Holiday. The East Room is a grand, formal space utilized by the president of the United States for important bill signings, speeches, and other public events. Judging from the ornate chandeliers and fancy drapes covering the windows, few would guess the East Room served as the laundry room for Abigail Adams in 1800 or the bedchamber and office for future explorer Meriwether Lewis as he served as an aide to President Thomas Jefferson in 1801.

Some two hundred years later, the East Room stood ready for a ceremony to celebrate the life of Dr. Martin Luther King. Rows and rows of small chairs had been arranged to face the stage, which had been placed near the rear of the room where President Bush would sign a proclamation honoring Dr. King's life and legacy.

I had arrived early to stake out a good spot to observe the activities in the corner of the East Room. Both the president and Secretary Card frowned upon White House staff that hung around events in which they had no official role or responsibility, but given that this was a federal holiday and that many on the White House staff had the day off, I figured that my presence wouldn't ruffle any feathers.

After the guests had taken their seats, Mrs. Coretta Scott King and her family arrived to thunderous applause. And then the loudspeaker announced: "Ladies and Gentlemen, the president of the United States." Wearing a blue shirt with a bold red tie, George W. Bush entered the room with a broad smile upon his face.

One would hardly recognize this president of the United States from the caricature created in the media. Often portrayed as being indifferent to the concerns of people of color and being uncomfortable in their presence, the real George Bush was quite the opposite. Making his way to the front of the room, the president's smile never wavered, and he looked rather pleased to be honoring Dr. King in the same room where President Lyndon Johnson had signed the Civil Rights Act into law in 1964 and handed Dr. King the pen.

After the applause died down, Mrs. King and members of her immediate family drew close to the podium with the president. In a touching ceremony, Mrs. King and her children presented the president with a portrait of the civil rights leader to hang in the White House. Depicting Dr. King with his arms clasped before him and a steady gaze upon his face, the portrait was greeted with cheers and applause from the guests gathered in the East Room.

Standing before a short wooden lectern with the seal of the president of the United States emblazoned upon it, Mr. Bush began his remarks by thanking his guests for coming. Looking at Dr. King's family, the president noted, "Mrs. King, thanks for this beautiful portrait; I can't wait to hang it." The president then turned somber and reflective as he remarked upon the significance of events that had taken place in this room with Dr. King some forty years prior:

On a summer night in 1964, right here in the East Room, President Lyndon Baines Johnson signed the Civil Rights Act and handed a pen to Martin Luther King Jr. The law marked a true turning point in the life of our country. As Dr. King put it, the Civil Rights Act was the end of a century of slumber.

More laws would be needed, and more would follow. But on that day, our federal government accepted the duty of securing freedom and justice for every American. Standing in the White House, marking a national holiday in Dr. King's memory, we are now two generations and a world away from Montgomery, Selma, and Birmingham as he knew them.

As I observed from my perch in the corner, I couldn't help but smile as I watched the president and the guests seated before him. Many elderly and distinguished-looking folks were in their seats and listening to the president in rapt attention. Sharply pressed suits for the men and brightly colored dresses with matching hats for the women seemed to be the dress code for the day.

Listening to the president's remarks and observing the audience before me, I was overcome by a strong sense of wonder. Just forty years ago, the United States was in the midst of a civil rights movement that would ensure that all Americans would be treated freely. Free in the right to vote, free in the right to attend the school of their choice, and free to work in the occupation of their choosing.

Forty years ago, it would have been unheard of for a young black man to be serving as a special assistant to the president of the United States. Even more unheard of would have been the composition of the president's cabinet and members of his senior staff. In 2002, America had a black national security advisor, a black secretary of state, and several black senior members on the president's team.

From a historical perspective, forty years is but a wink of an eye. But in that short period, much of Dr. King's dream had been achieved. The fact that I was standing in the corner of this grand room and celebrating Dr. King's life with a roomful of others was living proof that King's vision and call for equality and justice had taken hold of the American consciousness. There was still much more work to do, but I couldn't help but marvel at how far we had traveled as a country in such a short span of time.

I turned back to the president, who was nearing the end of his prepared remarks.

"Here on all the roads of life," said Dr. King in a sermon, "God is striving in our striving." As we struggle to defeat the forces of evil, the God of the universe struggles with us. Evil dies on the seashore, not merely because of man's endless struggle against it, but because of God's power to defeat it. Martin Luther King Jr. lived in that belief and died in that belief.

Some figures in history, renowned in their day, grow smaller with the passing of time. The man from Atlanta, Georgia, only grows larger with the years. America is a better place because he was here, and we will honor his name forever.

As the assembled group burst into applause once more, the president signed a proclamation commemorating the Martin Luther King Jr. Federal Holiday 2002. A glorious end to a glorious ceremony, I thought, as I slipped out of the room. I could hardly wait to see where the portrait would hang once the day's ceremony had concluded.

As it turned out, I had to wait a lot longer than I imagined to view Dr. King's portrait upon the wall in the White House. Several months following the East Room ceremony honoring Dr. Martin Luther King, I found myself one evening walking back from a meeting in the East

Wing of the White House to my office in the USA Freedom Corps. Scanning the large color photographs of President Bush in various scenes and settings of his presidency, I started to wonder where the King portrait had been placed.

Leaving the East Wing and walking through the ground floor of the residence of the White House, I marveled at the portraits of the former first ladies. *Wouldn't be here,* I thought. Continuing through the colonnade and past the Rose Garden, I made my way inside the West Wing itself. *It's got to be in here, somewhere,* I reasoned. Walking past the famous four-panel Norman Rockwell illustrations "So You Want to See the President" that had been drawn for the 13 November 1943 issue of the *Saturday Evening Post,* I decided to look in the ground floor of the West Wing and work my way up through the building. But to no avail.

I decided to ask Secretary Card if he had seen the Dr. Martin Luther King Jr. portrait. Like me, the president's chief of staff had assumed the portrait would be hanging up somewhere in the building but had not caught sight of it. A week or so later, though, he told me that he had solved the mystery of the portrait's whereabouts. Apparently my inquiry had piqued Card's interest as he told me he had searched around the White House complex himself and could not locate the portrait. He directed the staff to track it down, and the portrait had been found in a storage facility where it had been housed shortly after being received by the president from the King family.

This revelation didn't entirely surprise me. As mentioned previously, both the president and the vice president receive thousands of gifts from foreign leaders and other dignitaries. Many of theses items are cata-logued by the White House Gift Office before being sent out wherever it is that such things are warehoused.

Card assured me that the portrait was on its way back to the White

House where it would be immediately hung for viewing. After thanking me for bringing the matter to his attention, Card asked if I could recommend a good place for the portrait to be hung. Reflecting for a moment, I answered that King's portrait should be placed near the door in the East Wing, as this is the entrance used by the public when they participate in the public tour of the White House. King's portrait, I reasoned, would be one of the first objects viewed by the public when they entered the White House. Card promised me he would see what he could do.

True to his word, I was happily surprised to leave a meeting with my colleagues in the White House Legislative Affairs Office when I was stopped dead in my tracks: Dr. King's face gazed down upon me from the wall. Looking over to the uniformed officer of the Secret Service who was seated nearby, I asked him when the portrait had been hung. "They just put it up," he answered.

Heading back over to the West Wing, I was simply thrilled. Rather than shrug his shoulders about the portrait's whereabouts, Andy Card had taken a personal interest in ensuring it was returned and placed upon the walls of the White House where it belonged. Moments like this made me realize why the president had chosen Andy Card to be his chief of staff. Now, schoolchildren and other visitors to the complex would observe the fallen civil rights leader's image in a place of honor as they toured the People's House.

Imagine, then, my reaction several months later in May 2003 when I found myself in the East Wing and absentmindedly looked up at the wall expecting to meet Dr. King's gaze. Instead, I was greeted with a colorful picture of President Bush and Philippine President Arroyo during her recent state visit to the White House. *What's going on?*

Wheeling around to the Secret Service agent seated at the desk behind me, I asked what had become of Dr. King's portrait. "I don't know," he replied. "Maybe they just moved it somewhere else in the building," he continued. I was so stunned and mad I could hardly speak. Who would have taken this down and why? Was it merely hung elsewhere in the building or had it been sent back into storage?

Retracing my steps of nearly a year ago, I sought to contain my anger as I went on the hunt for Dr. King's portrait once again. Same as before, King's portrait was nowhere to be seen. I had to think about my next steps rather carefully.

On the one hand, the logical choice would have been to march right back to Card's office and tell him that King's portrait was missing once again. On the other hand, Andy Card had his hands full with managing the staff and issues for the president of the United States. As sympathetic as Andy had been when I raised the issue initially, I just didn't feel comfortable going back to him again; Card had enough things to worry about at the moment.

A few days later, I had my answer: Linda Gambatesa. Gambatesa serves as the deputy assistant to the president and the director of Oval Office Operations. A close confident of Card's, "Linda G." was always there for me when I needed a bit of advice on how to navigate tricky situations. This was one that certainly qualified.

Reaching out to Linda, I relayed the events surrounding the King portrait's discovery and subsequent disappearance. I told her that I didn't want to bother Secretary Card on the matter again, but I wasn't sure what to do. Linda G. told me she would check with the White House Curator's Office and see what she could find out.

As it turns out, the portrait had been mistakenly taken down and sent off to storage once again. What Linda G. didn't tell me, I heard from a confidant of mine in the chief of staff's office: Card himself had let it be known that the portrait was not to be moved again *under any circumstances* without express advance approval from Card's office. Before long, the portrait was soon back up and hanging in its spot on the wall in the East Wing.

Like all good stories, this one has a happy ending. Early in 2004, Coretta Scott King and her son, Martin Luther King III, asked to meet with President Bush. The Domestic Policy Council Staff placed King's scheduling request through the system, and it was granted. As a result, the DPC would brief Andy Card and perhaps the president himself, in advance of the meeting. Kristen Silverberg, the president's deputy domestic policy advisor, asked if I could join the initial meeting with Card, Coretta Scott King, and MLK III just prior to their visit in the Oval.

As we settled into Andy's spacious office just steps away from the Oval, I was awed by the air of dignity and grace with which Mrs. King carried herself. After a few moments, Card ushered her down the hall to meet with the president while a few of us remained to speak with MLK III and Mrs. King's chief of staff, Lynn Cothren.

About half an hour later, Mrs. King returned to Card's office where we had remained. Card had arranged for his assistant, Christal West, to take Mrs. King on a quick tour to the East Wing. Looking over at me, Andy said, "Ron, perhaps you'd like to walk with the Kings and show them the portrait?" We both knew that this was unnecessary as Christal was already going to take the group over. Instead, this was just another example of how Andy Card went out of his way to treat me with respect and courtesy: He knew I would love to accompany Mrs. King and wanted to ensure I got the chance.

Walking through the Rose Garden with Coretta Scott King was a surreal experience. She was a charming and engaging conversationalist. I told her my grandparents lived in Valdosta, Georgia, and that my mother had been born there as well. Passing through the residence and toward the East Wing, we discussed my background and my particular duties in the White House. Rounding the corner and headed down the hall to the spot where Dr. King's portrait was hanging, I was excited to see how Mrs. King and her son would react to the portrait of their husband and father.

As we drew near, Mrs. King and her son fell silent. Walking up to the portrait and gently tracing her finger along the picture frame, Coretta Scott King spoke in a tone that was little more than a whisper and barely audible: "That's my Martin," she said. "That's my Martin." Silently nodding my head, I remained in silence as the family gazed at King's portrait. What an unforgettable experience and honor to have shared that special moment in time.

"Dear Secretary Card"

THANKSGIVING 2002. MY FAMILY AND I GATHERED AT MY brother's house in Boca Raton, Florida, for an extended holiday to celebrate one of the few times in the year when we are all together in the same place at the same time. During my stay, I was asked about my new job at the USA Freedom Corps and what it was like to be a special assistant to the president of the United States.

I regaled my folks with stories from briefings in the Oval Office, and they checked out the loot I had brought home from the gift store bearing the seal of the president. My parents looked like children at Christmastime tearing into their Air Force One windbreakers and squealing as they tried them on. My brother and sister-in-law were equally pleased with Air Force One blankets, courtesy of the U.S. Air Force Airlift Command gift shop.

Over the course of my stay, we spoke about the inroads I had made as far as minority outreach was concerned. My parents offered suggestion after suggestion about places the president should go and people he should visit. As we chatted in the kitchen, my brother called out from the living room: "Ron, you might want to come take a look at this." On the screen before us, Senate Majority Leader Trent Lott hovered above Senator Strom Thurmond as the senator from South Carolina participated in a celebration marking his one-hundredth birthday. I asked my brother what the big fuss was all about.

Almost as if I had been heard through the television, CNN replayed the footage once again. In the coverage, Senator Lott noted that his home state of Mississippi was one of four that Strom Thurmond carried in his unsuccessful bid for president in 1948. At that point in history, of course, Mississippi was strongly opposed to integration. But Lott wasn't finished. He followed up by saying, "We're proud of it. And if the rest of the country had followed our lead, we wouldn't have had all these problems over all these years, either." Whoa!

What did Lott mean by "we're proud of it"? Was he proud that Mississippi had stood for cross burnings, lynchings, and the like? For that matter, did he mean that if the rest of the country had followed their despicable lead, the United States wouldn't have had any "problems" with those uppity . . . I was stunned. For the rest of the evening, I monitored coverage on the 24/7 cable outlets looking for statements of condemnation from Republican leaders in the House and Senate. For that matter, what was the president going to say about this?

One day stretched into another, and the silence was deafening from the Republican leadership regarding the comments of the Senate majority leader. For his part, Lott remained secluded at his home in Mississippi, lamely attempting to duck the media. This outrage *must* be addressed, I thought.

As more and more time elapsed, Lott and his supporters grew bolder and bolder. Offering a weak attempt at damage control, Lott said, "This was a mistake of the head or of the mouth, not the heart," echoing a line used by Jesse Jackson in 1984 when he referred to New York City as

"Hymietown," a comment which many interpreted as being anti-Semitic. You know things are bad for the Senate majority leader when he has to resort to quoting Jesse Jackson as a defensive measure.

The final straw was when I checked my White House voicemail one evening. I had received a call from a noted black activist in Jackson, Mississippi. The woman whom I had met earlier in the year while delivering remarks in Mississippi had called to ask if I was willing to come to Jackson to participate in a rally of black Republicans in support of the embattled Trent Lott. "We really need you, and Trent really needs you," she said. I couldn't believe it: A black woman was asking me to go to the heart of Dixie to march on the State Capitol to show support for a seemingly racist man who said he opposed integration? That was just too much for me.

My family, meanwhile, was pressuring me from the other side. My parents wanted to know how I could support the Republican Party when the Senate majority leader had uttered such a terrible remark and hardly any of his colleagues had made a peep? Worse still, my parents wanted to know how I could support President Bush and work at the White House for a man who had refused to repudiate Lott's remarks. Great. I was pressed by my folks, who were furious the Republicans had not tossed Lott out on his ear, and black Republicans in Mississippi who urged me to rally to Lott's defense.

The Trent Lott incident forced me to confront my own beliefs as to why I chose to identify myself politically as a Republican. I certainly hadn't chosen to be a Republican to fit in or take the popular political route as a black American.

I also wasn't a Republican due to the eloquence and dexterity in which Republican Party officials had tried to appeal to blacks. Other than the occasional silly speech about ours being the party of Abraham Lincoln, I hadn't heard anything up to that point that made a compelling case to blacks to desert the Democratic Party in droves. Instead, I chose to be a Republican due to the party's platform on fiscal responsibility, promoting a strong national defense, and education, just to name a few issues.

Sadly, I felt the party had done a relatively poor job in trying to explain why other folks of color should feel comfortable or welcome as Republicans. The fumbling and bumbling of the Lott incident would only reinforce negative images about the Republican Party toward blacks at a time when little substantive steps were being taken in my mind to diversify our ranks. This was unacceptable. The longer prominent politicians did nothing to condemn or criticize Senator Lott for his remarks, the deeper the damage we would sustain as a party.

I wanted and waited for the president to speak out. I felt prolonged silence would only serve as acquiescence to Lott's remarks. From my vantage point of working on his staff and observing him from up close, I knew that the president wasn't a racist—to the contrary, he is a caring and thoughtful person to people of all faiths, nationalities, and colors.

In fact, I was initially attracted to Governor Bush as he was the first Republican politician running for president in my lifetime who had seriously attempted to tackle the issue of making serious inroads into various ethnic communities. Bush had spoken repeatedly during his first campaign for office about his vision of "compassionate conservatism," a concept where he envisioned people would achieve greater success in life through the benefits brought about by a strong educational foundation, lower taxes, and the ability to own their own home.

And yet, I never had the impression that Republican Party officials or leaders on Capitol Hill fully understood what the president was trying to do then or now: Bush looks at people of color as individuals, rather than a monolithic demographic constituency whose members all think with one mind and speak with one voice. More succinctly, most Republican politicians have no clue that folks like Jesse Jackson or the Reverend Al Sharpton do not speak to the dreams, aspirations, and struggles of black folks any more than one white politician could possibly represent all of the competing interests of white people from different walks of life. I had been eager to join Bush's White House team as I felt he would reach out to people of color and stress to all Americans that his policies and initiatives were appealing due to their substance, rather than promising particular programs that would appeal to one ethnic group or another. At the same time, I could not remain a part of a team that did not forcefully condemn the comments of the Senate majority leader that appeared to endorse the dark, racist days my grandparents and parents had rallied against so that my brother and I would be able to attend school, vote in elections, and purchase a home without fear of racial prejudice. I had to do something.

As I returned to Washington D.C. following my holiday break, I was bubbling over with emotions. What exactly should I do? With Mary Matalin's departure from the president's staff several months prior, I didn't have my usual sounding board. Then I decided to take a gamble: Chief of Staff Andy Card always had told us we could knock on his door day or night if we really needed him. Mulling my options, I decided I would write Card a letter and follow up with his scheduler in a few days to arrange a time to meet.

"Dear Secretary Card," I began. After several attempts at trying to sound professional and analytical, I composed a letter to the president's chief of staff straight from the heart. I told him how upset the Lott incident had made me and how it made the Republican Party look bad since efforts to rebuke the senator for his comments had been lukewarm at best. We looked like the Dixiecrat Party rather than the party of

Abraham Lincoln. That was just unacceptable to me. After placing my unfiltered thoughts and emotions on paper for nearly two pages, my task was complete. I printed out my final document on the heavy, formal stationery with "The White House" emblazoned in bold, blue type. Hand-delivering the letter to Card's personal assistant that night, I had no idea how it would be received or acted upon.

The next morning, I returned to my office and booted up my computer. No e-mails from the West Wing and no phone messages to greet me, either. Had I made a mistake? I wondered if Card had even read my letter. Hour after tortuous hour, I heard nothing. Going home after work that evening, I wasn't sure what I should do next. I couldn't shake the feeling I had made a terrible mistake in writing Andy Card such a personal letter.

Feeling a little down, I called my dad and told him about what I had done. He told me he was very proud of the fact I had had the courage to write the White House chief of staff and speak my mind to him on such a sensitive topic. He assured me that few people would have ever done such a thing, and he was confident Card would reply to me either in person or respond in kind with a letter. My spirits were somewhat lifted, but I went to bed that night wondering what the next few days would have in store for me.

Switching on my light in my office the next day, I noticed my voice-mail light was illuminated. I was startled to hear an unmistakable voice with a clipped New England accent greet me. "Hi, Ron," the message began. "This is Andy Card, and I received your letter," he said. Here goes nothing, I thought.

Card told me that my letter had upset him a great deal, and he wanted me to see him. He asked me to arrange with his scheduler to get in to see him as soon as we could arrange it. Shortly thereafter, I found myself walking down the first floor of the West Wing, headed for the office of the chief of staff.

Entering his suite of offices, I was immediately greeted by my old friend, Melissa Bennett. "The chief will be right with you, Ron," she told me.

The door opened as I heard, "Ron Christie, please come on in here." As I walked through the door, Card strode over to greet me and shook my hand. A short man with a ruddy yet friendly face, Card was an interesting contradiction in personalities as the White House chief of staff. On one hand, he was quiet, unassuming, and fiercely loyal to the president. The first person to greet the president in the Oval Office each morning and often the last staffer out the door at night, Card was the consummate insider and powerbroker.

On the other hand, unlike many of his predecessors in the job, Card genuinely cared about the health and welfare of the White House staff. Not just the inhabitants of the West Wing—on more than one occasion I had spied the chief of staff sitting down with more junior staff and career government employees in the cafeteria in the basement of the Old Executive Office Building. Card was well liked and deemed fair by all who met him.

Just the same, I felt nervous as I settled into the chair he gestured to. Special assistants to the president do not often have one-on-one meetings with the chief of staff, particularly not to discuss how badly the Republican Party had misplayed its hand. As I gathered my wits to speak, I was disarmed by a wide grin as my eyes rose to meet his. Before my nerves got the better of me, I threw caution to the wind and told the chief what was on my mind and on my heart.

I told him we looked bad because the Democrats have always accused the Republican Party of being racist and insensitive to the concerns of black people. I shared with him the feelings of pride, joy, and honor my parents had felt that their youngest son worked for the president of the United States. All that being said, my parents wanted to know what *I* was going to do about the fact that the head of the Republican Party had been silent about Lott's comments.

I took a step further out on my narrow branch to tell Card that we could do much better by making inroads with persons of color who viewed the president and his administration with skepticism, if not outright hostility. I used my mother as an illustration to make my point. My mother, a college-educated registered nurse, prides herself on being fair and objective. That being said, I told him, my mother, a resident of Florida during the 2000 presidential election, believed that the Republicans stole the election and suppressed the rights of African Americans to vote in the state. "Sir, if I can't convince my own mother that Republicans care about black people with her youngest son working for the president of the United States," I told him, "we're in for a world of hurt."

"What do you think we should do?" he replied. I told him that we should stop treating black people like black people. Republican politicians make the mistake of traveling into black neighborhoods and talking about crime, welfare reform, and vowing to take the drugs off the street. Instead, "Let's talk about tax reform, school choice, and home-ownership," I ventured. "The more we start treating folks like they're Americans rather than African Americans, the better off we'll be." I wasn't finished just yet. "Another thing that disturbs me is that we seem to have 'black' events around here. Rather than bringing in the gospel choir to sing and sway in the East Room during Black History Month, can't we do something else? Can't we do more than pander to the religious folks who come in here, sing, and then start criticizing us the second they leave the building?" I implored him.

"Instead, let's have the president visit with small business leaders, doctors, and investors who support the president's vision and also happen to be black. This will send a shot across the bow that we're not going to pander to the establishment any longer." As I spoke, Card kept his eyes fixed upon me. He let me go on for nearly twenty minutes before I finished what I wanted to say. Now came the moment of truth.

Looking me dead in the eye, Card took a deep breath and said, "I never really thought about what you had to say before. No one's ever said anything like that to me." Uh-oh. "As you know, I'm originally from Massachusetts, and I don't have much experience with being black," he said matter-of-factly.

"These issues are very important to me, and they are very important to the president. If I could ask you, Ron, would you serve as my conscience for these types of issues? Would you tell me what we're doing right, what we're doing wrong, and how we can do better? I would like you to do this either in person or drop me a note if there's something you want me to look at. If you ever think you and I need to talk, you just tell Melissa you and I need to talk and we'll schedule it." Wow! To say that I was elated was a major understatement.

Card and I then bantered back and forth about life in general before Melissa stuck her head in and said the president was expecting him in the Oval Office. With a cheerful smile and a wave, Andy Card gathered his notebook and headed for the door. Before he left, he turned around and said, "I'm *so* glad you felt comfortable enough to share this with me." And with that, he was gone.

I walked back to my office and called my parents to tell them what had happened. They were thrilled, and so was I. In the months that followed, Secretary Card and I would converse time and time again about ways in which the president could make incremental inroads with constituencies that might have suspected both Mr. Bush's sincerity and commitment to diversity.

More than lending a sympathetic ear to my frustrations about how the administration's message was being received around the country, Card became an active participant and devoted significant amounts of his time to find ways in which the president's agenda could resonate with those who were skeptical about his policies.

While our initial discussions concerned specific outreach efforts the president should consider in the African-American community, our conversations were not limited strictly to racial matters. For example, I was eager to return to the White House to meet with Card following an encounter I had in Kennebunkport, Maine, with a local merchant who expressed his displeasure with the president's perceived insensitivity to their economic woes. I had been invited to Augusta, Maine, to deliver a speech on volunteerism along with Governor John Baldacci. Following my speech, my fiancée, Jennifer (now my wife), and I decided to head to the coast to enjoy a romantic weekend in Kennebunkport. As we walked around Kennebunkport, we ventured into a rustic, local bookstore called Kennebookport to scan the latest titles. A clerk behind the counter had pleasantly asked us where were visiting from, and I responded, "Washington D.C." The clerk took that as an opening to launch into a stern lecture on how President Bush didn't understand the needs of local folks there in Maine, despite his statements on the need to grow jobs and strengthen the economy. Did the president have any idea what was going on up here? Before I could answer, he continued by telling me that the local paper mill was about to close down and more than two thousand people would lose their jobs. How, the gentleman wanted to know, did the president's jobs plan affect factory workers from the local paper mill who would soon be looking for work?

As I wasn't an economist, I didn't want to launch into a specific defense of the president's economic agenda. Instead, I replied that I was certain the president had a keen eye out for what was going on in Maine and other communities around the country that were transitioning from factory to high-tech jobs. Providing educational and financial assistance could help retrain workers to compete for jobs that they currently did not have the proper training for.

After we left the bookstore, I knew I had to speak with Card and alert him to the concerns I had heard. If one gentleman could politely express his frustration to me about the president's perceived insensitivity to the demographics of the local economy, chances were there were others who harbored similar thoughts.

Returning to the White House after a pleasant weekend in New England, I made a mental note to stop off to see the chief of staff and brief him. As it turned out, I caught Card sitting at the staff table in the White House Mess shortly thereafter, and I related the story that I had heard in the local bookstore. Unbeknownst to me, Card, a native of Massachusetts, had spent many a summer vacationing in Maine, and he knew the area well. Thanking me for my report, Card promised that the information would be put to good use, and I have no doubt that it was.

Anecdotes like these only help to illustrate why the White House staff is so loyal to the president and to his chief of staff. Unlike stories from friends in previous White Houses whose unsolicited advice was discouraged, Andy Card implemented an open-door policy that encouraged us to reach out and share our thoughts. Were it not for his warmth and genuine concern for people, I would never have dreamt of sitting down to compose a heartfelt letter that started with the words "Dear Secretary Card." I'm glad that I did, as it allowed me to establish a relationship with someone who greatly enhanced my White House experience as he constantly challenged me to think of ways in which the president could best serve the American people.

We are all extremely fortunate the president has chosen Andy Card to have his hand on the rudder to set the course for staff in the White House and the Executive Branch to follow. You couldn't find a more honest or dedicated public servant to do the right thing for all of us.

All Good Things
Must Come to an End

IN THE FIRST FEW DAYS FOLLOWING THE PRESIDENT'S FIRST inauguration, Secretary Card warned us that the lifespan of a policy aide in the White House was rarely longer than eighteen months. Doing the people's business in the People's House is a 24/7 occupation, and downtime was often a luxury and an exception, with work intruding on every aspect of life each and every day. Even now, I jump involuntarily when I hear a cell phone ring or a Blackberry buzz: Who could it be now? Did something happen?

After nearly three and a half years in the White House, more than twice as long as the average lifespan of a West Winger, I knew it was the proper time for me to go. For my entire professional career, my instincts always told me when it was time to move on to another challenge and another occupation. I had achieved far more from a personal and professional standpoint than I had ever dreamed at the White House.

Who would have ever imagined that I would be able to brief the vice president on budget and tax issues or walk slowly through the colonnade of the Rose Garden with the president as we discussed an upcoming set of remarks he was about to give in the East Room? Whether submitting briefing memoranda or conducting briefings with some of the most intelligent and powerful people in the world, I had pushed myself to the limit and kept my head above water without drowning under the immense pressure I felt every minute of every day.

And while I felt I was at my personal pinnacle at the White House, I just knew that my time to serve was nearing an end. Initially, I was excited to serve as the acting director of the USA Freedom Corps after Bridge's departure. I was eager to remove the "acting" from my title and run the office and put my stamp on the president's service initiative.

Getting over the ego of wanting *my* office or *my* stamp on things, I realized that I had done something far more important while on the USA Freedom Corps staff: I was part of an amazing team that had helped the president help the American people who wanted to serve a cause greater than themselves by volunteering in their communities in America and around the world. Interest in the AmeriCorps program had grown dramatically, and more young people than ever were looking for opportunities to engage in public service.

As for the Peace Corps, the agency had nearly placed more volunteers in more countries around the world than at any period of time since President Kennedy created the program back in the 1960s. Indeed, our initial band of carpenters on Jackson Place had helped build a foundation for renewal in public service that will stand long after President Bush has left his office. I had no reason for regret, and instead I felt that I was honored and privileged to have been part of something that was truly special.

Still, my decision to leave was not an easy one. It had taken me several years to get to the top of my professional game, and I was reluctant to walk away. The president of the United States respected my opinion, as did the vice president and key staff such as Andy Card and Karl Rove.

While never entirely comfortable briefing the president, I had gotten over my sense of fear and awe and was able to respond when he challenged me on a particular point or asked follow-up questions without losing my composure.

From a professional standpoint, what job could possibly be as exhilarating or challenging as serving the president of the United States? I couldn't imagine that briefing a law partner in the conference room could be quite as exciting as briefing the president of the United States in the Oval Office.

From a personal standpoint, I had made some amazing friendships and worked closely with some of the most intelligent and capable people I have ever met. Through the good times and the most difficult of times, these folks were always in the trenches with me. And yet for me, it wasn't enough to stay any longer.

Tony Snow's edict on White House service never warned me just how physically exhausting gearing up to go to work each and every day could be. I had made so many emotional withdrawals from my mental piggy bank with hardly any deposits of meaningful rest or relaxation to build up my reserves that I found myself burned out with little more to give. Perhaps there are jobs out there where you can go to work and consistently operate in a fog, but serving on the White House staff isn't one of them. The president and the American people should have energized staff that are willing to dedicate 100 percent of their time, energy, and effort to the job. I just didn't have enough gas in the tank any longer.

After agonizing for weeks over my decision, I finally sat down at my computer and drafted my letter of resignation to the president. In a few simple paragraphs, I thanked the president for the opportunity to serve in his administration and help build the culture of service, citizenship, and responsibility that the president felt so strongly about.

Putting the finishing touches on my letter, I inserted a sheet of official

White House stationery into the printer and inserted the document in an envelope to hand-deliver to Andy Card. While I slowly made my way to the West Wing, the letter in my inside jacket pocket felt as heavy as a brick. I was disappointed to find that the chief was not currently in his office. Not willing to return with the letter in my pocket once again, I handed it over to my friend, Jared Weinstein, one of Card's assistants.

"No, Ron, don't do this. I can't accept it," Jared began. While I knew he was mostly kidding, I was touched by his desire not to see me go. Just the same, I had made up my mind, and I wanted Card to deliver my letter to the president for me.

Walking back to Jackson Place, I felt as if a huge weight had been lifted. While I was reluctant to leave the White House, my family and I had discussed the matter at great length, and I was making the best decision for me both professionally and personally. When I reached the office, I heard my phone ringing incessantly on my desk.

Picking up the receiver, I heard Jared's voice on the line asking me to come back to the West Wing: Andy Card had read my letter, and he wanted to discuss it with me immediately. Back down the stairs and over to the White House I went once again. This time, the chief was in his office, and he didn't look entirely happy to see me.

Shutting the door immediately behind me, Card invited me to sit on the couch as he took a seat in the chair directly opposite me. Unlike many of our previous conversations, I knew this was not going to be an easy discussion for me. With no preamble, Card told me that he didn't want to accept my letter and, launching into a very spirited discussion, told me I was doing an amazing job and he didn't want me to leave. I responded that I had thought about this for a long time and that I had put off my resignation for a few months to ensure continuity in the Freedom Corps Office with Bridge's departure.

Rather than exert pressure on me to stay, Card merely asked that I take the weekend to reconsider my decision. If I felt as strongly about leaving on Monday or early in the next week, Card would submit my letter to the president. Shaking hands as I turned to go, I promised him Jennifer and I would discuss my decision once again.

Early the next morning, Jennifer and I were awakened to the sound of my cell phone ringing. Who in the world could that be? As soon as the cell phone stopped, the home phone started up. I knew immediately that this had to be someone from the White House trying to track me down. Sure enough, answering the phone, I heard a voice say: "Please hold for Harriet Miers." Harriet, then serving as the president's deputy chief of staff, had called to say that the chief had told her I had submitted my letter of resignation and she wanted to see how firmly my mind was made up.

I was flattered by her outreach, but after Jennifer and I had revisited my decision the night before, my resolve was firm: It was time for me to go. I told Harriet that I appreciated everything that she and the chief had done for me, but I knew that the time was right for me to step aside—Jennifer and I were about to get married, and I was ready to accept a position at Patton Boggs, one of Washington D.C.'s premier law firms. Harriet thanked me for my service at the White House and promised to tell the chief my decision to leave was solid.

19 March 2004. Waiting in the Roosevelt Room with my parents and Jennifer, my mind was a kaleidoscope of thoughts and emotions. What does one say when it is finally time to say goodbye? As the heavy door opened, Blake grimly greeted me with a smile and patted me on the shoulder. This wasn't going to be easy.

The Oval Office was ablaze with color that afternoon as we walked through the narrow door and across the hardwood floor. I stepped off to the side to allow Jennifer and my parents to pass as the president strode over to greet us.

My parents and Jennifer were brimming with happiness and pride for me: Their smiles and laughter lit up the room. After shaking hands with my family, the president asked that I step forward in front of his desk—the very desk under which JFK Jr.'s playing had been forever immortalized in *Life* magazine when his father was president—to take a departure photograph for me to have as a memento of my time in the White House.

After we posed for a few photographs, the president looked me dead in the eye and told me: "You're a good man. I'm proud of you for everything you've done here." I was touched, and for once in my life, at a loss for words. I was overwhelmed with emotion by his words of praise and didn't want to say anything for fear my voice would betray me.

As if sensing this, the president suddenly reminded us all that Jennifer and I were just about to be married. He continued our visit by exclaiming: "The wedding party—I want a picture with the wedding party." Back to the *Resolute* desk we went, and the president posed for a few more shots.

"Mom and Dad. I want a picture with Mom and Dad." My parents floated over, and he posed for a few more pictures. He wasn't done just yet. "Everybody. I want a picture with everybody!" Everyone went over and posed for one last shot with the president before our special moment in the Oval was over.

Just before we left, the president spoke the same words to my parents that still ring in my ears to this day: "Your son's a good man. He's done a great job, and I'm proud of him." While the president may have been proud of me, I was proud to have been a part of an amazing team, an amazing group of dedicated people who worked long hours for relatively little pay.

Rather than seeking monetary rewards, most of us who served in the George W. Bush White House—particularly after the September 11 attacks—served for a different reason and a far better purpose: We loved our country and wanted to serve a cause greater than ourselves. As contrived as that might sound, no truer words could be spoken—we wanted to help the president serve the American people.

Now my time to serve had ended, and the most difficult walk lay before me. My parents and Jennifer let me depart the White House complex the same way I had arrived over three years ago: alone. Leaving my identification badge behind in the hands of White House Personnel Office Director Caroline Swann, I walked down West Executive Avenue towards the black iron gates for the last time.

As I neared the Secret Service agents posted at the gate, I took a deep breath and walked forward. "It's my last day," I offered. One of the agents walked forward and said, "Mr. Christie, thank you for your service, sir." My eyes started to well. The agents buzzed me through, and I pushed open the gate and pulled it closed for the last time.

Standing on the outside looking back towards the White House, I thought of the words with which President Bush had challenged the staff on his second day in office: "[To] begin the work we were hired to do and leave this a better place than we found it." I could honestly say that I had completed the work I was hired to do and hoped that my service, in some small way, had left this magical place a little bit better than when I had found it years before. With tears of happiness in my eyes, I turned away from my memories and slowly walked away to rejoin my family: We had some celebrating to do.

Acknowledgments

I AM UNABLE TO PUT INTO WORDS MY SENSE OF AWE AND gratitude to have been presented the opportunity to serve this great country—first on Capitol Hill and next within the White House. There are thousands and thousands of bright, capable, and dedicated people who are eager to serve in our government at any moment, and precious few positions are available to do so. Fewer still are the positions on the staffs of the president and vice president of the United States.

As far as writing this, my first book, I cannot express sufficient gratitude to David Dunham, the publisher of Nelson Current. David, thanks for taking a chance on this project and believing that there is strong interest for a book about the presidency of George W. Bush that is positive and honest. Thanks also to Joel Miller, my editor at Nelson Current, who went the extra mile to ensure this book made it through from start to finish.

And particular recognition must be shined on the most amazing literary agent, Joseph Brendan Vallely, whom I am proud to call a friend. Never taking no for an answer, Joe V. shared my vision for this book, one many in the publishing community were unable or unwilling to see: Most Americans like President Bush, and they like to see a positive vision of the president as a strong leader and a decent man.

My deepest gratitude to my parents, family, and friends for your love and patience you've shown me all these years. Without your backing and support, none of this would have ever become a reality. Just saying thank you doesn't nearly seem to be enough, but thank you a million times over.

And about the amazing woman to whom this book is dedicated, what can I say? You are the most demanding critic, copyeditor, and stickler for detail. Every sentence of every paragraph of every chapter in this book has had the benefit of your eagle eyes, counsel, and brilliant mind. I love you, Jennifer Kay, for being my best friend, soul mate, and inspiration for living. Without you, the world would have little meaning. With your love and support, the world is the most amazing place, and ours is the most amazing life.

Index

Abraham, Spencer, 10, 94

Adams, Abigail, 257

Adams, John Quincy, 48

Addington, David, 21–22

African American, xviii–xix, 66, 68, 75–76, 111, 114–16, 122, 207–9, 223, 276, 278

Allen, George, 3, 8, 15–16, 174

Ambrose, Stephen, 56–59

AmeriCorps, 170, 174, 186–97, 199, 207–8, 217, 284

Armey, Richard K., 190–93, 199

Associated Press, 90

Atkiss, Steve, 226

Atwater, Lee, xi

Baldacci, John, 278

Bartlett, Dan, 132, 219, 221

Beamer, Todd, 150

Bennett, Melissa, 179, 275, 277

Black History Month, xviii, 116, 276

Bohrer, David, 103

Bolton, Josh, 241

Bridgeland, John, 39, 45, 140–41, 143, 171–76, 179, 186–87, 190–93, 195–97, 199–200, 216, 219, 222, 235, 247, 284, 286

Bush, Barbara, 150

Bush, George H.W., 22, 25, 30, 54, 114, 150

Bush, George W., ix–x, xvii–xx, 3–7, 9, 11, 19, 25, 28–29, 31, 35–36, 38–39, 49, 58–59, 65–66, 73, 75–78, 87–88, 97, 102, 116–17, 121, 134, 136, 150, 153, 168, 178–79, 189–90,

193–95, 197–99, 201, 207–8, 211, 215–19, 222–28, 231, 236, 243, 250, 252–53, 257–58, 261, 264, 271–73, 278, 289

Bush, Laura, 225–27

Bush v. Gore, 6

Card, Andy, x, xvii, xx, 25–28, 36, 40, 48, 160, 176–83, 197, 200–1, 206, 235, 240–41, 243, 247, 257, 261–64, 273–74, 277, 279–80, 283–84, 286–87

Carter, Jimmy, 150

Carter, Rosalyn, 150

Carville, James, xiii

Chao, Elaine, 232, 250, 252

Chavez, Linda, 13–14

Cheney, Liz, 103

Cheney, Lynne Vincent, 31, 102–4, 122, 150

NELSON CURRENT

NELSON CURRENT

A Subsidiary of Thomas Nelson, Inc.

Nelson Current, the political imprint of Thomas Nelson, Inc., publishes probing, engaging, thought-provoking titles that explore the political landscape with audacity and integrity. With a stable of news-making writers including both veteran journalists and rising stars, as well as *New York Times* best-selling authors such as Michael Savage, Nelson Current has quickly established itself as a clear leader in the ever-expanding genre of political publishing.

Check out other provocative, relevant, and timely books at NelsonCurrent.com.

White Ghetto
How Middle Class America Reflects the Decay of the Inner City
1-59555-027-5

In this provocative book, Star Parker proves that the sexual chaos, values disorientation, and social turmoil we see in our inner cities is merely a more sharply focused picture of moral collapse in mainstream America. Covering today's hot-button issues, Parker argues that wealth and infrastructure have cushioned the collapse in the 'burbs, but the disease is the same and only waits for the support structures to falter and fracture before ghetto culture hits the family down the street, or in your own house.

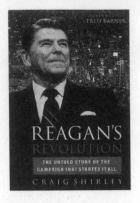

Reagan's Revolution
The Untold Story of the Campaign That Started It All
By Craig Shirley
0-7852-6049-8

This is the remarkable story of Ronald Reagan's failed yet historic 1976 presidential campaign—one that, as Reagan put it, turned a party of "pale pastels" into a national party of "bold colors." Featuring interviews with a myriad of politicos, journalists, insiders, and observers, Craig Shirley relays intriguing, never-before-told anecdotes about Reagan, his staff, the campaign, the media, and the national parties and shows how Reagan, instead of following the lead of the ever-weakening Republican Party, brought the party to him and almost single-handedly revived it.

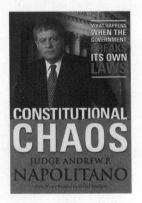

Constitutional Chaos
What Happens When the Government Breaks Its Own Laws
By Judge Andrew P. Napolitano
0-7852-6083-8

In this alarming book, Fox News commentator Judge Napolitano makes the solid case that there is a pernicious and ever-expanding pattern of government abuse in America's criminal justice system, leading him to establish his general creed: "The government is not your friend." As an attorney, a law professor, a commentator, a judge, and now a successful television personality, Judge Napolitano has studied the system inside and out, and his unique voice has resonance and relevance. Napolitano sets the record straight, speaking frankly from his own experiences and investigation about how government agencies will often arrest without warrant, spy without legal authority, imprison without charge, and kill without cause.

What people are saying about Nelson Current books:

Bill O'Reilly

about Judge Andrew P. Napolitano's *Constitutional Chaos*

"This book will open your eyes."

Ann Coulter

about Richard Poe's *Hillary's Secret War*

"This book is required reading."

Sean Hannity

about Jesse Lee Peterson's *Scam*

"[A] bold prescription to make America a better place."

Rush Limbaugh

about Star Parker's *Uncle Sam's Plantation*

"[This book] casts new light on the redemptive
power of freedom."

Glenn Beck

about Jayna Davis's *The Third Terrorist*

"When you read this book, you are going
to be convinced that it is the truth."

Sam Donaldson

about John McCaslin's *Inside the Beltway*

"Whether you are a Democrat or a Republican,
you will love this book."

Neil Cavuto

about Barry Minkow's *Cleaning Up*

"[This] one-of-a-kind story makes for indispensable reading."

George Will

about Craig Shirley's *Reagan's Revolution*

"This is an exhilarating story of political daring."

Hugh Hewitt

about Ben Shapiro's *Brainwashed*

"A brilliant new voice for a generation of activists."

Michael Medved

about Rebecca Hagelin's *Home Invasion*

"[O]ffers a persuasive, common-sense voice that demands
respect—and attention . . ."

Robert D. Novak

about Tom Coburn's *Breach of Trust*

"This book provides a rare, invaluable portrait of life
as it really is on Capitol Hill . . ."